Our Debt to Greece and Rome

EDITORS
GEORGE DEPUE HADZSITS, PH.D.

DAVID MOORE ROBINSON, PH.D., LL.D.

GREEK ART

THE BASIS OF LATER EUROPEAN ART

BY

ARTHUR FAIRBANKS

COOPER SQUARE PUBLISHERS, INC.

NEW YORK

1963

Published 1963 by Cooper Square Publishers, Inc.
59 Fourth Avenue, New York 3, N. Y.
Library of Congress Catalog Card No. 63-10265

TO MY STUDENTS IN ART
AT DARTMOUTH COLLEGE
WHOSE INTEREST AND COÖPERATION
GAVE FORM TO THIS ESSAY

CONTENTS

[vii]

LIST OF ILLUSTRATIONS

In Text

At End of Volume

GREEK ART
THE BASIS OF LATER EUROPEAN ART

GREEK ART

THE BASIS OF LATER EUROPEAN ART

I. THE APPEAL OF GREEK ART

IN ANY large art gallery or museum the visitor is presented with various types of art. He may see contemporary paintings, sculpture, furniture, utensils and decorations, objects familiar to him, as well as the work of the Renaissance from which later Europe has drawn its inspiration; he may see fascinating objects from little known civilizations; sculpture from India, paintings from China, textiles and metal work with intricate Persian or Moorish design are set before him, only to attract while their strangeness almost repels him; and he may see the sculpture, the frescoes and vase paintings, the utensils of ancient Greece and Rome. It is evident to one who watches the visitor that only the art of Greece and Rome makes an appeal like that of modern art, an appeal to which he immediately responds. It is nearer to us than any other art in its form and in its spirit. Instinctively we accept it as our own, though it was created in a distant age and in a foreign environment.

The debt of later European art to Greece is universally recognized. The student may analyze the classical tradition in art in order to determine its essential characteristics; he may seek to follow the influences which were set in motion in Greece, as they grow weaker or are modified by other forces or again are revivified by fresh contact with the legacy of ancient Greece; he may investigate the significance of art in Greece as compared with its significance in later European life; he is not called on to prove the self-evident thesis that our art is deeply indebted to that of ancient Greece.

A few examples will suffice to show that art outside the classical tradition is foreign to our eyes, as that of ancient Greek is not. Passing over the art of uncivilized peoples we may glance at two examples from Central America, small gold amulets from Costa Rica. The first is the figure of a man with short body, flattened arms, and stumpy legs; long locks of hair represented by curved parallel lines project from each side of the head and end in spirals; the fingers are indicated by parallel lines which join in a curve at the base of the palm; and the toes, long straight parallel lines, are all there is to make the foot. The second is a fantastic creature, a bird with wide-spreading tail, cres-

FIG. 1a. GOLD AMULET FROM COSTA RICA

cent-like wings, and a head with enormous beak, flanked by thin ornaments which suggest each an animal's head with huge mouth containing rows of teeth, while yet another head, that of an animal, projects from what should be the body. There is no direct effort for representation. Rather, the artisan has selected forms in nature which he could adapt to his weird design, a design no doubt guided in a measure by fancies connected with his spirit world. He uses curved lines and spirals freely in building

[5]

up his designs; he takes little account of natural proportions, but suits his proportions to his artistic purpose; his conventions are as foreign to us as is the meaning he doubtless sought to

FIG. 1b. GOLD AMULET FROM COSTA RICA

express. Long examination of such figures may or may not convince us that they are examples of genuine art, but a glance is sufficient to show that they are not our art and that our art owes no debt to them.

These early developments of culture on this continent disappeared, leaving practically no contribution to the life that has succeeded them.

Civilization, as we know it today, has developed in two main streams, one from its source in India spreading out over China and the East, the other spreading westward from its fountain head in Greece. The life, the thought, and the art of the East are hardly less foreign to us than the prehistoric culture of America.

Take for example a copper figure from southern India, representing Siva dancing. Of course the features and the accessories are unfamiliar to us, and the refinement of the slender limbs is not what we expect in sculpture. The four arms seem only a monstrosity. The flying hair, the forced curves of the garment, the contorted attitude may give graceful lines; but at first sight we find them meaningless and fantastic. Is there any artistic significance, we ask, in the child on which this strange figure is dancing? Nor is it any less at variance with our conception of art as the free product of the artist's imagination, when we find that this type with only the slightest variations persists for centuries.

Indian sculpture does not aim to represent nature with accuracy; it does not seek to produce forms more perfect than nature; it is never satisfied to depict mere physical beauty. It is

[7]

FIG. 2. COPPER FIGURE OF SIVA

not the expression of the artist's individual experience, except as he experiences for himself the efforts of his age and his race to interpret Being, Being which is unlimited by individuality and time and space. It is a hieratic art, holding close to traditional details which at length are explained in an elaborate treatise, since every detail is full of meaning. It is a transcendental art, for it finds its content in the inner consciousness, and its truth is judged by metaphysical and imaginative standards. It is a symbolic art, which cannot be appreciated without such knowledge of the devotional and philosophical ideas that the beholder may respond to the intent of the artist. Its sincerity, its truth of feeling, its spiritual meaning, are what make it a great art. In intent and in procedure it is alien to our eyes till long study reveals its significance.

The art of China and Japan is a development or outgrowth of the art of India in much the same sense that later European art is the legacy of Greece. The hieratic art is greatly modified by the genius of China and of Japan, but its nature and its method are fundamentally similar. And when the Chinese artist turned from distinctly religious subjects to landscape, his art is still in a manner foreign to the Greek tradition. He does not deal with a material, mechanical world, simple to us because we think we know the forces controlling it; the world is still for him the passing expression of eternal spiritual Being. He does not seek to reproduce with detailed accuracy the forms and shades of color visible to the eye; rather he depicts a beauty suggested by what he sees, but created by him as more perfect, more graceful, more instinct with feeling than the accidental combination of facts which he actually does see.

In the Ming landscape here reproduced, the mountain rising above the mist, the curving waterfall and its spray, the gnarled tree, the bold rock, and the path with one man walking and another seated, are in no sense literal representations of physical fact. It is the height of the mountain, the force of the rushing water, the massive ruggedness of the rock, the wildness of the whole scene which the artist felt; and he depicted not what he saw, but what he felt. In a sense the painting presents the higher truth, the ideas evolved by the artist of the underlying meaning of what he saw, and its perfection is an ideal perfection of beautiful design and form which he created. Such a

FIG. 3. MING LANDSCAPE

[11]

landscape is alien in conception and significance to the art of our western civilization.

If we turn to the early art of Mesopotamia and Egypt, we are in a world totally different, but hardly more akin to our own. True, it is an objective art, dealing with facts and not with symbols; true, the Greek race learned much from these earlier civilizations with which it came in contact, and made them more intelligible to us by what it learned from them; but this early sculpture and painting and decoration are certainly not our art.

Take for example the tomb relief representing the royal treasurer Nofer, an Egyptian relief from the period of the pyramids at Gizeh. Its proportions, especially the long body and the short upper legs, are not normal. The legs are in full profile, the body up to the armpits in three-quarters view, just showing the back of the small right hip and leaving the left breast in profile, the shoulders in full front view, and the head again in profile. The curves of the legs, the body, and the arms are rather mathematical than natural. The relief is so low that the figure is hardly more than drawn in sharp outline, except for the simple, startlingly sensitive modelling of the face.

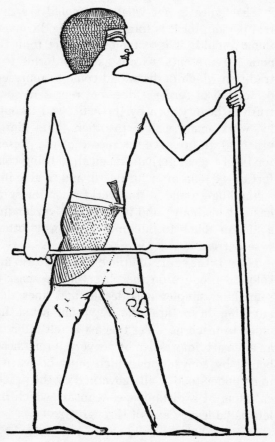

FIG. 4. NOFER, ROYAL TREASURER

The figure is not what one would see in a real person, for it is forced into a rigid conventional mould; it is not more perfect than the man it represents, except as it conforms to a tradition which perhaps had come to represent perfection of form; it does not represent some truth or beauty seen by the artist and through his work made visible to others. Its aim is practical, to preserve the record of the present for future ages; perhaps magical, to bring comfort to the man after his death, and to give him a standing-ground in this world when the spirit has left his body; and it is decorative, lending a human touch to buildings or utensils otherwise barren.

If art is the effort to utilize line and form and color to produce on the observer the sense of something simpler and deeper and finer than anything in nature, the Egyptian artist has much to teach us. Yet this art is felt today as an alien art, impressive by its very foreignness; bound by conventions which must be learned to be understood at all; governed by the practical aims of a distant age — an art which has left us no legacy except through Greece.

* * *

IT remains to consider the converse of the proposition that has been under discussion: namely, that the art of the ancient Greeks, distant as it is in time, is immediately felt as our art. The furniture, the utensils, and the decorative arts generally of Greece are not foreign to our eyes. The drawings on Greek vases of the fine period, except for the strangeness of silhouette figures on a red background and of reserved red figures on a black background, are not foreign to us, even though the economy of line and the absence of any attempt at shading may seem unusual. And the paintings that have survived, for the most part late mural decorations or late reproductions of paintings by artists of the best period, are not out of line with our conception of painting. These pictures, like many of the subjects depicted on Greek gems, have an immediate interest today for children as well as adults. Can anything be more vivid than the hunting scenes and war scenes on some of the Mycenaean gems, to go back to a period from which the Greeks learned much. It is enough for our purpose, however, to speak only of sculpture, considering a few typical examples chosen to illustrate the whole range of sculpture from the late sixth century

[15]

B.C., when Greek art began to find itself, down to the first century B.C. when it was modified to meet the foreign demand of Rome.

I

THE so-called "Apollo" of Tenea (Plate I), found near Corinth, dates from the latter half of the sixth century B.C. The rigid pose of the figure, standing squarely on both feet and with both hands hanging down close to the body, the full breast, the narrow waist and the large thighs call to mind the Egyptian type of standing figure which continued unchanged for thousands of years. The Greek statue, however, though it may have been influenced by the Egyptian prototype, does not show a fixed conventional rendering. In the first place, the interest of the artist in what he saw is evident in his efforts to reproduce it. He is not particularly successful in handling the muscles of the arm and the lower leg, or in his treatment of the kneecap and the ankle and the mouth, but he has studied them and he is trying to show what he sees. And secondly, though he is not bound by any rigid convention, the artist renders what he sees in terms of a felt design, much of it a design of simple mathematical curves.

The lines of the eyebrows well down on to the bridge of the nose, the outline of the shoulders as seen from the front, the bulging muscles of the limbs, the line that bounds the abdomen below the midriff, the lines of the groin, are almost exactly arcs of circles, while the crown of the head is all but a hemisphere. True, these curves are distorted in any but a frontal view, but evidently the figure, though finished all around, is intended to be seen only from the front.

This felt pattern, this vision of the human form in terms of an ideal design, can only be understood as an effort to translate the facts of life into terms of artistic perfection, which, here incipient, found its fruition a century later. Both the effort for true representation and the effort for something truer and finer than mere representation, differentiate Greek sculpture even at this stage from the kinds of art considered earlier in this chapter and mark it as what western civilization has understood to be art.

II

PERHAPS half a century had passed before bronze workers of the Aeginetan school were called on to cut marble figures for the pediment of the temple of Aphaea. The theme was the victory of Greece over Troy, prototype in heroic legend for the victory of Greece over Persia. One of these figures (Plate II) represents a nude youth hastening forward to catch a falling comrade who has been wounded. The progress in the artist's knowledge of the human figure is amazing, inconceivable except for a race devoted to athletic contests and made familiar with the nude form by constantly seeing it in these contests. In fact the deficiencies of these figures are mainly due to the conscious effort of the artist to show by a dry severe treatment his knowledge of the athlete's frame and muscles. His aim is to represent what he saw in all its rich detail.

Yet these figures without garments and most of them without protecting armor were not what one actually saw in battle, any more than the Homeric descriptions of these battles in hexameter verse can be regarded as bare, literal accounts of warfare. Moreover, the simple design of the Apollo of Tenea has here been replaced by a rich and more complicated design, which by every line reinforces the idea of the figures. The flowing lines of the body and left leg in themselves give the feeling that this youth is rushing forward to catch his companion; while the bent right knee gives him firm support, and the extended arms complete the idea of a person poised for action. Certainly the artist is intent on representing what he sees; but the sense for design, the vision in terms of a pattern which at every point reinforces the meaning of the figure till the observer feels as well as sees the crouching youth, this is the mark of Greek art which later Europe has accepted as its standard of art.

III

THE statue of Athena (Plate III) is a marble copy of a bronze statue, presumably the Athena not wearing a helmet which Pheidias made for the Lemnians in the middle of the fifth century and which they dedicated as a votive offering on the Athenian acropolis. It is the figure of a mature young woman, looking down at a helmet which in the original she carried in her right hand and holding a spear erect in her left hand. She wears a heavy woolen garment which falls in severe folds to her feet, and an aegis on her breast, while the thick curls of her hair are confined by a broad fillet. The effort for accurate representation is no less evident than in the statue just discussed. With in-

creased knowledge and skill the artist has depicted this young woman as one might see her,
a being instinct with life and strength; and the
garment is represented almost literally, in a
way that does not wholly conceal the full form
of the body underneath. Nor is there any less
effort for design than before, in the charming
pose of the figure, the head slightly bowed and
turned, the hair that frames but does not shade
the face, and the carefully studied planes of
the face itself. The loose clinging folds of the
garment above the concealed girdle, the varied
line of the lower edge of the overfold, the severe columnar treatment below, broken only
by the bent knee, and the almost too rigid arrangement of the edges down the right side
where the garment is open, all these bespeak
the artist's thought of the design in which he
saw the figure.

A new element, however, has come into the
foreground. Here we have not mere representation of the physical form, but also representation of the human spirit informing the
body and manifest in it. If the question is
asked, How can the sculptor depict the inner
life and spirit in his work? the only answer is
another question, How do we ever know the

spirit and character of a man from his face and his bearing? as constantly we feel we do. In this instance we seem to see not merely a living woman, but a person of poise and dignity, a woman mistress in her own sphere and skilled in the activities of her life. She is entirely free from selfconsciousness, in that her mind is completely absorbed in the life outside herself and in the work that lies before her.

Does the simplicity of this face, unmarred by any suggestion of portraiture, seem cold, not quite human, perhaps too perfect for any living being? Does it lack that touch of human intimacy, which sometimes is so appealing in the face of the best Egyptian statues of the Old Empire? Such is the idealism with which the Greeks conceived their gods as human yet super-human beings, a conception which gave the artists of the fifth century B.C. their great opportunity. The aegis on the breast of this figure proves that she is the goddess Athena. Her dignity, her majesty characterize the goddess of wisdom, mistress of the arts of peace as well as of war, the embodiment in divine form of the practical, the intellectual, and the civic life of Athens.

The art which represents the beautiful spirit,

the divine spirit, in and through the beautiful body, we instinctively recognize as the forerunner of our religious art.

With the fall of the Athenian Empire in 404 B.C. a great change in Greek life reached its consummation. The strong civic life which had characterized the city-state and which had reached its highest expression in the Athens of Cimon and Pericles, a civic life which gave large scope to the individual while at the same time it absorbed his energies in the state, a civic life with high and satisfying ideals, now lost much of its potency. And art, which had been wholly a civic affair, became more and more a vehicle for the expression of individual sentiment.

IV

THE Hermes of Praxiteles (Plate IV), found in the Temple of Hera at Olympia where the Greek traveller Pausanias saw it in the second century A.D., is the one extant original which can confidently be assigned to one of the six greatest Greek sculptors. Though it was not one of his celebrated works, the existence of modified copies indicate that it was not unknown or unrecognized in antiquity. It is the

[22]

figure of a nude young man standing on his right leg with the left foot drawn back, and leaning on a tree trunk from which hangs his garment. On his left arm he carries the infant Dionysus, who is reaching up for some object, perhaps a bunch of grapes, which Hermes held up in his right hand. He is not looking at the child, though his head is slightly bowed, but gazes over it out into space with a vague, unseeing expression, only half conscious of the playful boy on his arm.

One primary interest of Praxiteles, as of his predecessors, was the effort to represent the human form as one might see it, if only a being of such perfect form ever existed. The bone structure, the firm muscles developed by athletic exercises, the soft skin, all are shown with a technical skill developed through generations and with a knowledge gained from scenes in the palaestra. The figure of the athlete in action or at rest had been the theme of every Greek sculptor. It remained for Praxiteles to depict the athlete, or rather the young man trained both in body and in mind, in a state of complete relaxation, yet with no trace of flabbiness or any physical weakness; it is the vigor of fine manhood completely at ease, which is

presented to the spectator. And this youth is
very much alive. The aim of the Greek sculptor to produce a figure instinct with life is em-
phasized in Greek story, beginning with the
tale of Daedalus whose statues could actually
walk. The meaning of such stories is clear as
one looks at this Hermes, which one must see
as a living being.

Nor does the representation stop with the
living physical frame; for the artist uses the
body to depict the mind, the human spirit of
his subject. Here it is not a mind absorbed in
the life of the community, but rather a mind
turned in on itself; not a mind controlled by
purposes of activity, but rather given over to
passing moods, a mind absorbed in meditation
that is near to melancholy. The whole figure
as well as the face suggests an attitude toward
life which tended to prevail in the Athens of
the fourth century B.C., an individualistic,
sometimes emotional, often introspective attitude.

The design is such as to reinforce the idea,
and to create immediately the feeling which the
relaxed dreamy figure presents to the eye.
From whatever angle it is seen, the long gentle
curves combined in a restful design produce

the impression sought by the artist. As one goes around the figure, it is not perhaps equally successful from every point of view, yet the same feeling persists in the ever-changing outlines, for the artist no longer conceives his work as to be seen from only one point. And as one looks away from the outline to the play of light on the surface, the broad planes merge in a unified whole which in itself creates the feeling of a living being relaxed and at rest.

With all its grace, charm, and expressiveness this Hermes sometimes strikes the observer as cold and distant. Certainly it lacks any touch that suggests portraiture, any of the little peculiarities that exist in every individual. If it is a being outside the sphere of daily experience, too free from imperfections to be human, if it is a pure idealized figure, the purpose of the artist is entirely clear. He is representing a divinity whose divine nature is nothing more or less than the perfection of humanity. It is a very human god, playing with a baby, introspective and wistful, looking with wonder on a complex world which stirs but does not satisfy his soul, like the youth of Athens at this time; yet it is a god.

An art which can transfigure human nature

[25]

into the divine by idealizing purely human traits, makes an immediate appeal to us.

V

It will suffice to speak more briefly of three later Greek statues which illustrate much the same characteristics, in types widely different from those already considered.

The Nike of Samothrace (Plate V) commemorates the naval victory of Demetrius Poliorcetes in 306 B.C. It is a Winged Victory blowing a trumpet, and poised on a pedestal which has the form of a ship's prow. Though the head and arms are missing, the sculptor's idea is manifest in every line of this vigorous female figure, who bends forward slightly to meet the wind as she alights on the warship. It is needless to speak of the artist's mastery of material, and his complete knowledge of the human body as it is revealed by the clinging garments blown against the flesh. His aim again seems to be the representation of what the eye would see, if only such a being existed — the developed female form, the garments blown back and tossing in the wind, the soul thrilled by the elation of free movement. The abiding impression of the figure is its real-

[26]

ity; it is a living, moving, joyous human being, yet more than human in that its quiet power, akin to the unconquerable forces of wind and wave, is the symbol of victory brought by the goddess.

At the same time it is not photographic representation, either of the body or of the garments. A thin robe does not take these fine, carefully arranged folds in any wind, nor does a thick mantle fall in these grouped masses of smaller folds, with such long sweeping curves. The confused restlessness of the garments is studied to produce just the effect the artist sought; in fact there is really no trace of confusion or of any restlessness except what the theme demands. Every line and plane is so handled as to bring unified meaning into the complicated design. It is this design which makes the figure so real. It is the design which brings life and motion and buoyancy into the figure, which takes up the subject and brings it home to the observer till he too is thrilled as is the joyous being in marble.

Granted that the artist's aim is to represent reality, yet he deals not with the individual but with a reality underlying the individual, not with accidental but with abiding truth, not with

what one does see but with what one may see
under his inspired guidance. For art to take
a familiar theme like this, a woman with garments blown back by the wind, and fill it with
new, satisfying meaning has ever been the goal
of our western art.

VI

THE Dying Gaul (Plate VI) was one of a series
of statues set up by Attalus, king of Pergamon,
about 230 B.C. to commemorate his victory over
the horde of Gauls which had been ravaging
Asia Minor. The nude man, mortally wounded,
raises himself on his right arm, his right leg
bent as he struggles against faintness and pain.
It is not at all a portrait figure but a type of the
splendid, virile race which had finally been
crushed by trained soldiery, for Greek art was
idealistic in the sense that it expressed the underlying idea rather than any individual example of the theme. The artist suggests respect
for the conquered race, and thereby the greater
glory to the conquerors. The whole story of the
invasion by the Gauls is epitomized in this figure, a man who has fought bravely, has been
wounded to death, and in a last effort raises himself up from the ground for a moment before he

succumbs to the inevitable. If we find in it a hint of the tragedy of failure, if it inevitably stirs our pity for the defeat of such virile life, we should probably attribute it to the situation rather than to any effort of the artist to play on these emotions, for he has treated the subject with a breadth and restraint which lifts it out of the everyday world into the world apart as would a poet in writing a tragedy.

In this case again the appeal of the artist is based on the sense of reality in his work. In dealing with a type so very different from the ideal type familiar in Greek art, he shows no less care for perfect bodily form, while at the same time he emphasizes the characteristics of a foreign, barbarian race. The long, lean body, the sharply defined un-Greek features, the subtle suggestion of skin exposed to the weather and uncared for, the bristly moustache, the unkempt hair — all bring the " barbarian " vividly before our eyes. The treatment of the hair, like the treatment of the garments in the Nike of Samothrace, is a good example of what is meant by representation in Greek art. There is absolutely no reproduction of detailed fact; at the same time there is a clear expression of just what the artist saw which conveys the sense of reality he desired. The method may be roundabout, the result is the vivid presentation of the visual facts.

And here again the design is such as to bring home to the observer the subject represented. The very lines of the figure, every line, in themselves suggest a mighty effort against overwhelming odds, an effort which inevitably ends in failure. While the gentle sweeping lines of the Hermes suggest physical and mental relaxation, and the masses of curves in the Nike are grouped in a unified pattern that expresses vital energy akin to the wind which plays with her garments, in the case of the Dying Gaul broken lines and sharp angles and hard planes constitute a design which reinforces the theme and in itself produces the feeling which was in the mind of the artist.

When the story of a great event is epitomized in a single figure and presented to us with such vividness that differences in time and space and social conditions disappear, we immediately claim the statue as our art.

VII

IN the great social and intellectual changes which mark the closing period of Greek supremacy, art changed profoundly. The sculptor tried new subjects such as pastoral scenes and other scenes from everyday life, while athletic figures were handled in such wise as to exaggerate the size or the hardness of the muscles, and myths like the story of Laocoön or Dirce were presented with all the horror of which the subject was capable. Moreover, the method of the artist was different; the effort even in the Dying Gaul for perfection of the human figure was no longer controlling.

A striking example of this change is found in the statue of an old woman carrying her baskets of vegetables to market (Plate VII). Her form is bent with age, her face sunken over toothless gums and wrinkled deeply, her feet gnarled and worn. No mark of age or poverty which would help to make clear the sculptor's intention is lacking or is softened to render the figure less repulsive. At first sight it is only this emphasis on reality which connects this statue with those that have already been considered as characteristic examples of Greek art, as though one quality only of the earlier work had persisted to the exclusion of all others.

While the differences from distinctive Greek work are not to be minimized in the least —

both the intent and the execution belong to an age which already was ceasing to be Greek — it should be noted that even here we are not dealing with a literal portrait. The artist is interested in the type; all that belongs to the type, the peasant features, the uncared-for skin, the sordid ugliness of poverty, are depicted with no redeeming grace; but it is the type with all its picturesqueness which claimed the attention of the Greek. To this extent only there is a touch of Greek idealism.

Moreover, the artist still depends on design to lend magic to his work. The folds of the garment which conceals the body would almost contradict his purpose, did they not create the feeling of a decrepit person holding her balance successfully though with difficulty, as she walks laden with her heavy basket. The pose of the figure, as well as the arrangement of the garments and the accessories, produces a design which itself gives the feeling of age in its struggle with poverty.

Can we not say that the changes which modified Greek art in its last period simply anticipated some of the changes in the legacy from Greece, which took place in later European work?

To resume: In primitive art and some developments from it the impulse seems to be a kind of magic, as when the hunter seeks to bring game under his control by fashioning pictures of the animal he is to hunt, or when the image of some god is thought to make present the god himself. And sometimes the impulse seems to be just the expression of the play instinct, the instinct to use line and form and color simply for pleasure in doing it. Whatever the motive, primitive art has left no direct legacy to our European civilization.

Nor do we claim the art of India and China and Japan as ours. In a sense it is mystical. It uses forms from nature only as symbols. Its significance is drawn from the mind of the artist and from the mind of the race as grasped by the artist. Its legacy to our civilization is only distant and indirect.

And the art of Mesopotamia and the art of Egypt we do not recognize at once as ours. These forms are strange to us; the conventions are not those to which we are accustomed; the aims are essentially practical rather than aesthetic. What we owe to them has come through Greece, transformed and re-created by the Greek spirit.

[33]

On the other hand the art of Greece we recognize at once as akin to our own. It is a human art, its primary theme the living, thinking, feeling human form. Its aim is through the human form to represent the meaning of the world, and the meaning of life. Such is the conception of art which in the main has determined the development of art in later Europe.

II. THE GREEK TRADITION:
ITS CONTENT

THE message of Greek art to later generations is the message of the Greek people. This small, gifted folk looked out on a world which to them was old and new, old with the achievements and discoveries of Egypt and the Near East, new with significance which they grasped and interpreted for succeeding ages. While the foundations they laid for science are hidden by the vast structures which have been built on them, in philosophy and in the fine arts we still look to Greece for inspiration. In all the various fine arts the task of Greece was to perfect if not to discover a technique which is still the standard by which technical success is judged, and then to use that technique to express a richly developed humanity. Though later times have modified in some directions and carried farther the forms of Greek technique, it is only in the greatest periods of European art that insight into the meaning of life has found the adequate expression which it did in Greece. Later Europe owes its conceptions of art to Greece.

Such statements are self-evident for the art of literature. We, like the Romans, find our prose models in Greek prose; from Greece we get our types of epic and lyric and dramatic poetry. Of the influence of Greek architecture traces are found in the buildings of almost any village street today. For sculpture and painting and the decorative arts, however (that is, for the field of the present volume), the case is not so clear. There is no single, clear-cut line of tradition from which one age might deviate but to which a succeeding age returned with new enthusiasm; moreover, in these forms of art the types are more fluid, more imaginative, less easily defined by simple categories than in the case of literature or architecture. Can we say that the sculpture and painting and so-called industrial arts of later Europe owe a large debt to Greece? Is there in fact a classical tradition still valid for these arts?

An examination of the problem yields some definite results of varying degrees of significance. In the first place it is easy to discover the appearance in our art today of subjects and designs and types which we inherit from Greece.

Wherever they originated, such elements of design as the maeander, the rosette, and other forms of ornament drawn from the vegetable world, and various types of scroll and wave and spiral patterns have come to us directly from Greece. We still copy certain forms of jars and pitchers, if not of furniture, from Greek prototypes. In our painting genre scenes, in less degree landscapes, and the not infrequent use of mythological subjects have a lineage that goes back to Greece. In the field of sculpture it is not difficult to discover example after example of modern work which repeats an ancient Greek type. When the mind of the young artist is concentrated for years on the remains of Greek sculpture, it is inevitable that his figures tend to take Greek proportions and even Greek features, and that not infrequently they repeat some arrangement and pose which was devised in Greece. The imitation is perhaps not slavish, as oftentimes in architecture, but its presence is none the less real.

The value of the artist's inherited stock-in-trade — elements of design, types of figures, subjects for his work — is sometimes questioned. If much of it came from Greece, such a legacy is of historical interest but in itself it has no great importance. On the other hand the very fact that the artist looks to Greek remains for his inspiration and therefore, consciously or not, adopts subjects and types from these remains, is clear evidence of our debt to Greece. In a word, our heritage from Greek art is no question of traditional details, however often they may appear; in sculpture, painting, and the decorative arts it must be sought in the very nature of our art and in the principles which govern artistic expression.

Secondly, many of the technical processes and formal devices of our art may be traced back to Greece. Consider so simple a thing as our metal coinage. Whether the Greeks invented what we know as coins — definite weights of precious metal of convenient size, which are guaranteed by a government stamp on obverse and reverse — or whether they adopted the device from another race in Asia Minor, it was the Greeks who made them works of art and from whom the use of coined money was passed on to Rome and thus to later Europe. The only change, other than loss of artistic excellence, has been the use of a milled edge, and the lowering of the relief to permit coins to be stacked in piles. The technical process of

[38]

cutting a coin-die was essentially the same as
that which had long been in use in Mesopotamia and in Mediterranean lands for cutting the
stone seals employed in sealing clay tablets.
The Greek sense for form and design, which
found expression in the sculpture of the fifth
and fourth centuries, was manifest even earlier
in this sculpture on a small scale — the cutting
of designs on small semi-precious stones to serve
as seals for their owners. Both the same mechanical process of cutting and in general the
same type of design were used for making
coin-dies. As for the subjects chosen for representation on coins, on the obverse was commonly the head or figure of the patron deity of
the issuing state, on the reverse at first just the
plain form of the punch head, later a device
with some further reference to the issuing city;
and it was not till the kings of Macedon were
conceived and represented in the form of a
divinity, as Alexander was thought of as a
Heracles and pictured as wearing the lion's skin
of Heracles, that we find on coins that portrait
of a ruler which became general in Rome and in
later Europe. It is merely a matter of history
that our coins are round and not rectangular as
in many parts of the East, that the devices on

them are heads and figures or symbols of the
issuing state, that the type of relief is Greek
rather than, for instance, the sunken relief of
Egypt — all because we derive our ideas of
coinage from Greece. But the fact that the
effort for a higher artistic standard in coins and
medals has always through the intervening
ages been inspired by the coins of ancient
Greece, is evidence that with the economic invention and the technical process we owe to
Greece here also an incalculable debt in the
field of art.

It is a question how far the processes of
making gold jewelry and utensils of silver and
bronze came to Rome and then to later Europe
from Greece. We know that the Etruscans
were expert metal workers, but we know that
their artistic designs were ordinarily based on
Greek models, and the technical processes
which were passed on to Rome may well also
have come from Greece. The shape of a bronze
pitcher, the free use of formal ornament engraved and repoussé, and often the decoration
of figured scenes in repoussé, were prized in
Rome and later Europe as they had been prized
in their Greek home. Apparently the processes
used in making artistic metal work were refined

in Greece, further developed by the Etruscans, and passed on through Rome to the European civilizations that have followed.

As for the processes of painting, one was Greek in origin. The Greeks attributed to Pamphilus of Sicyon the invention of encaustic painting, in which melted wax applied with a hot spatula was the vehicle for carrying the colors. Two earlier methods of painting, fresco painting (i.e., painting on a damp plaster ground with water colors) and tempera painting on a gesso ground, were highly developed by the Greeks and were passed on to the Roman world in the manner in which they had been used in Greece. We find no literary reference to inventions or discoveries of new grounds or vehicles, except hot wax, or colors for painting. We do know, however, from vase paintings of century after century that the Greeks went a long distance in discovering the possibilities of line drawing. The beauty and vigor of the outlines on vases of the best period, the use of " guiding lines " to suggest the third dimension, and the effects produced with extreme economy of means, have made these simple scenes a direct inspiration to later European artists. But the achievement of the Greek painters which has had the greatest effect on later European art was the introduction of chiaroscuro. Early painting in Egypt and Crete and the painting of the Greek masters through the fifth century was in flat color without shifting tones or any clear indication of light and shade. So long as painting was prized primarily as an adjunct of sculpture both in relief and in the round, the carved surface furnished all the play of light and shade that was needed. But when painting on a flat surface came itself to a place of honor, it was inevitable that the Greek interest in accurate representation should lead to the effort to represent light and shade. Far as earlier artists had gone in suggesting the third dimension by the skillful use of line, the time came when that was not enough to satisfy their desire. The introduction of chiaroscuro in painting is attributed to Apollodorus who was born at Athens toward the end of the fifth century B.C. The practice soon became general. Adopted by Rome and passed on to later Europe, it has become an integral part of what our civilization means by painting. In spite of the misuse of shifting tone which has led so many artists astray, in spite of the popular confusion of paintings with colored photographs, which has brought as a reaction new experiments with flat color, this complex instrument of chiaroscuro has in general set painting above sculpture as the most effective of the visual arts.

Another characteristic of western painting from the Renaissance on, is the effort to treat figures and other objects as existing in a space that envelops them. This atmosphere surrounding figures was of course entirely out of the question in the great fifth century paintings in which the subjects were sharply drawn and laid in with flat color. But in the fourth century such devices as the softening of the edges and shifting tones in the background began to be employed along with light and shade on the figures themselves. There is no effort for enveloping atmosphere in early eastern painting or in Egypt or elsewhere. The first efforts in this direction were made by Greek painters in their desire to paint figures as they saw them, though the possibilities of the idea remained to be worked out in later Europe.

Yet another device of late Greek painting is perspective in our sense of the term. In the Orient, so-called " vertical perspective " was developed in a manner quite strange to our eyes.

While it remained for the Renaissance to work out the scientific use of our " vanishing point perspective," the perspective which is the basis of our art of drawing and painting, the clear beginnings of it are found in extant mural paintings of the Graeco-Roman period. It is difficult to admit the claim of some scholars that our perspective began to be used by a scene painter like Agatharchus in the fifth century. But when we read that Pamphilus of Sicyon was a student of geometry and demanded of his pupils a knowledge of mathematics, it suggests the effort for perspective in his painting before 300 B.C. In the late mural paintings of landscapes and sometimes of architectural subjects our type of perspective is quite developed. Perspective as we know it may fairly be claimed as part of our debt to Greece, both because the beginnings of it are found in Greek painting, and because the scientific development of it in the Renaissance was inspired by the Greek desire for accurate representation.

It remains to speak of the devices which were developed by the Greek sculptor and passed on to later generations. Sculpture in very low relief, practically drawing in sharply cut lines on stone, had long been in use in Mesopotamia and in Egypt; and in Egypt a proportional reduction of the depth of the figure, especially of the face, had been developed in such wise as to secure modelling of great delicacy. It was left to the Greek sculptor to discover the possibilities of the reduction of the subject by planes to the depth of relief he desired to employ. Between the front plane of the greatest projection and the fixed back plane of the background, he introduced intermediate planes with delicately modelled transitions, which preserved the illusion of the third dimension without interfering with the two-dimensional design he had undertaken. Whether he was working on coins and gems, or on a grave relief or a temple frieze, the principle was the same. Partly by the study of reliefs on Roman sarcophagi but perhaps more by the study of Greek coins, men like Nicola Pisano and Ghiberti and Donatello found the value of this method and made it a principle for sculptured relief in Europe from the Renaissance on.

For sculpture both in relief and in the round the Greeks worked out devices for representing the figure itself, the garments, and such details as the hair, which became an important factor in the classical tradition. The far-reaching use of these devices is illustrated by a seventh century A.D. marble torso from China, now in the Museum of Fine Arts, Boston. The very use of marble for this figure, now almost universal for sculpture, calls attention to the Greek tradition, since the use of marble for statues, now so general, seems to have begun in Greece. The curves of the body and the pose are not Greek; but the transparent drapery laid in carefully systematized folds, and the heavier mantle over the shoulders betray their Hellenic origin. The garments on figures of the Gandhara school in India at a considerably earlier period are quite generally handled with the devices originating in Greece.[1] Similarly the hair on a Gandhara head in Boston,[2] though arranged in the Indian style, is carved with light wavy locks in the Greek manner.

But it is in our western sculpture that these methods of the Greek artist have been controlling. The very forms of the human body as developed in the later Greek canon have influenced our sculpture from the Renaissance down to the present time — the rather slender torso with developed chest and slim straight hips,

[1] Cf. Coomaraswamy, *History of Indian Art,* Figs. 90, 92.
[2] *Ibid.,* Fig. 94.

the fairly long limbs, the not too heavy bones,
the wiry muscles of the man trained in athletics
but not a professional athlete, such are the
forms which imposed themselves on the sculptors of the Renaissance and their successors.
The problem of treating hair in bronze and marble was solved only slowly in Greece. At first
it was only a wig marked in grooves and doubtless painted; then the artist learned to make
long curls and braids, and suggested locks of
hair by wavy lines radiating from the crown of
the head; and at length short hair was suggested by curling locks engraved on the almost
flat surface of the skull, as in the Charioteer at
Delphi. It was evident that hair could not be
represented with photographic detail, but the
impression of short thick locks could be reproduced by a sketchy treatment as on the Hermes
of Praxiteles or the Apoxyomenos, while the
effect of long hair in light thick strands was ob-
tained by a studied design of curling locks as
on the Lemnian Athena. Coins and carved
gems made known to Renaissance artists Greek
methods of treating hair long before the finer
examples of Greek sculpture were known to the
modern world. Again, the handling of garment materials and garment folds, varying

[47]

with the kind and thickness of the material, was studied with results that have persisted. The graceful lines, the grouping of folds into systems so designed that each fold takes its place in an easily understood and effective pattern, the use of this pattern to express the meaning of the whole figure, and the distribution of folds to bring out rather than conceal the structure of the body underneath — these are devices which served as a guide and an inspiration to later artists. It is only necessary to study the sculptures of the Parthenon to learn the achievements of Greek workmen in this field and to recognize the source of our modern conceptions of the use of the loose garment in sculpture.

Again, what may be called a principle of construction in art was developed in Greece and became a part of the legacy to civilizations that followed. A simple example of this principle is found in the decoration of metal and pottery vessels in western civilization, as compared with the decoration in parts of the world which have not been controlled by its influence. It has been suggested that the very forms of Chinese vessels make an emotional appeal, in contrast with the intellectual appeal of Greek forms. While this suggestion may not be accepted, there can hardly be any question that the nature and the arrangement of the design on Greek vases has a logical quality which in general has characterized later European design. In the case of a Greek water jar (hydria) each part of the painted or repoussé design is adapted to the form of the vase; on the spreading part there may be some narrow band or bands of ornaments; the bottom of the body proper perhaps has a band of long darts or flutings which seem to help support the main part of the body; marked off by some narrow stripe of ornament, the main decoration, some scene from daily life or from mythology centering on the front of the vase, is so designed as to emphasize the form of the vase itself; there may be another scene, a frieze on top of the shoulder, and some ornament with vertical trend on the mouth below the lip; the handle is probably fluted with perhaps some decoration at the point of junction with the body, and if there is some plastic ornament on a bronze vase, it finds its proper place at the junction of the handle with the lip. Each type of vase has a design adapted to its form and worked out in a simple logical manner in harmony with this form.

[49]

The subtle balance of form and color which gives distinction to the finer Chinese porcelains and the complex patterns engraved on Chinese bronzes illustrate a totally different principle of construction in design. Here every line has its meaning, every spot of color is felt to be in the right place, but the attempt to explain its rightness would be vain; it is intuitively felt to be right, a judgment of feeling and not of intellect. The importation into Europe of Chinese objects, particularly porcelains, in the eighteenth century introduced to European designers the eastern method of construction. Inasmuch as it was not really understood (or rather felt) by those who sought to imitate it, the result was on the whole disastrous. The scattered flowers and other ornaments on various makes of European porcelain which resulted from this oriental influence offer a marked contrast to the usual ordered (and often stiff) types of decoration which continued to prevail in England. And much of the ultra-modern decoration, for instance in textiles and wall coverings, seems vaguely to have a similar aim in its appeal to emotion, and in its revolt from an influence that ultimately came from Greece.

The contrast with the Greek intellectual

principle of construction is different but none the less clear in Saracenic decoration. The amazing mass of detail, mainly geometrical but with some motives from the vegetable world, is intriguing in its richness and delicate complexity. The inlaid wood, the carved stone, the engraved metal surface seem to vibrate with life. Wherever the eye rests, it finds one design merging in another, a device fatiguing to the intellect but stimulating to the emotions. Such ornament is occasionally found in European metal-work, but in general the Greek principle has guided our decorative arts.

Furniture may serve as another example of the Greek principle of construction. The bird's heads on the ends of chair arms, the animal's claws on the bottom of the legs, the vertical inlay on the legs of chairs and stools, and the horizontal designs on horizontal bars were a logical part of the structure. The ornament, painted or inlaid or carved, was selected with reference to the shape of the objects and to the place it occupied. It fulfilled its purpose only when it became an integral part of the object so decorated.

The same principle of intelligible composition is found in Greek sculpture and painting,

though in these fields it is less easy to demon-
strate. For sculpture in the round it is illustrated by the emphasis on the so-called Canon.
According to Chrysippus [1] Polycleitus worked
out a mathematical system of proportions for
the human figure, " of finger to finger, and of
all the fingers to the palm and the wrist, and of
these to the forearm, and of the forearm to the
upper arm, and of all these parts to each other."
Polycleitus not only wrote a treatise on this
subject, known as " The Canon," but also produced a statue, presumably the statue which
we know through marble copies as the Doryphorus (Plate Xa), which was also called the
Canon because it embodied the system of proportions described in the treatise. Euphranor
of the Isthmus and Lysippus changed the proportions chosen by Polycleitus, but laid no less
stress, we are told, on the "science of proportions " which they claimed to be the foundation
of their success in sculpture. This " production of beauty from a small unit through a long
chain of numbers " [2] is clearly an effort to explain the intelligible basis of composition, on

[1] Quoted by Galen, H. S. Jones, *Ancient Writers on
Greek Sculpture*, London, 1895, pp. 128-9.
[2] H. S. Jones, *Ibid.*, p. 163n.

which these artists laid stress. Nor can any-
one study Greek sculpture without recognizing
the clarity and definiteness of the design, the
way each line and each curving surface takes its
proper place in the unified composition of the
figure as a three-dimensional whole.

Further, this principle is clearly manifest in
sculptured groups, and particularly in the series
of figures which were set up in the pediments of
temples. The composition of pediment groups
is planned to satisfy the desire for unity by
means of a strict balance, yet with the maturity
of this art the double center of the Parthenon
pediments and the introduction of varied groups
at intervals from the center enabled the artist
to secure variety and interest without at all interfering with the sense of a logically unified
whole or of the dignity befitting a monumental
group.

A comparison of Greek sculptured friezes
with the kind of frieze found in pre-Greek art
sheds light on the point under discussion. For
example, the reliefs from the palace of Assur-
nazir-pal (*circa* 889–859 B.C.), which are now
scattered in American and European museums,
illustrate formal Assyrian art at its best. The
figures of the king, his attendants and the di-

vinities he worshipped, carved in very low relief but with vigorous sensitive lines, follow one another with practically no intelligible relation. It is a series of figures, each with its own meaning, but all very much alike and not combined into one structural whole. What a contrast even with the maidens in the procession on the Parthenon frieze, not to speak of other elements in that procession, where no two figures are alike and all are combined according to the Greek principle of structure in design. If one turns to the pictorial reliefs of Egypt, where there is no lack of variety in the figures or of interest in the scene, the relation which combines the figures in one common activity does not find expression in a corresponding unified design. Structural unity is lacking both in the individual scenes and in the connection between different scenes contiguous to each other. Perhaps it is desirable at this point to call attention to the sculptured friezes of Indian art, because they illustrate a principle of construction totally different from that developed in Greek art. Where a Greek frieze brought figures into an intellectual, logical relation and expressed the scene in a design which reinforced its meaning, the Indian frieze presents an emotional, mystical grouping of the figures.[1] Not that there is a lack of structural unity in the Indian frieze, but that the unifying principle is essentially so different from that developed in Greece and passed on to Europe, that it is foreign to our eyes.

The same principle of construction is found in Greek painting. Even a cursory survey of the mural paintings that remain to us, paintings of Greek themes and often based on Greek prototypes, reveals a striking likeness to paintings of the Italian Renaissance in the composition of the scenes. The architectural treatment of the walls and the practice of reproducing a garden or buildings as if they were seen between the columns of a portico naturally are not repeated in later easel paintings; but the pictures introduced into the panels, mainly mythological scenes, illustrate types of composition which are often paralleled in paintings of the Renaissance and later periods. Interesting as it might be to follow out these parallels, the results of such a study would often be misleading. There

[1] E.g., Coomaraswamy, *History of Indian Art*, Figs. 141, 165, 208.

is no reason to think that either Fra Angelico or Raphael or Velasquez was directly influenced by any surviving classical paintings. On the other hand the fact remains that the principle of clear and intelligible construction in design, a principle worked out in Greek art, was revived in the Renaissance and handed on to later Europe. It is this principle of structure which accounts for the likeness in composition between extant classical paintings and paintings of later Europe. In painting as well as in sculpture and architecture and the industrial arts, it is an important element in our legacy from Greece.

The subjects, the designs, and the types which later Europe has derived from Greece are a relatively unimportant contribution to our art; the technical processes and formal devices inherited from Greece are indeed an essential part of our heritage; and the Greek principle of construction as it appears in later art is a clear proof of our indebtedness to Greece. Yet none of these details, however significant, really expresses what we owe to Greece. Rather, our greatest debt is the conception of what art is and what it may mean in human life.

Our real legacy is to be found in the spirit of Greek art. When this is felt, guiding and spurring on artistic endeavor, the classical tradition is no dead transmission of outward forms, but it is instinct with the breath of creative life.

III. THE GREEK TRADITION:
ITS COURSE

BEFORE undertaking to study the Greek spirit in art, it is desirable to consider briefly the course of the classical tradition in Europe.   The outward form of the Greek tradition continued with but slight change in the Roman world. Statues and artistic metal work of every description were transferred by fleets of ships from a conquered Greece to Italy; the demand for this new kind of luxury was such that the supply was totally inadequate, and Greek artists were imported to copy masterpieces or to produce sculpture and painting for their Roman masters; artistic activity, which had languished in Greece, was revivified by the stimulus of this new demand both in Rome and in Roman commercial centers like Alexandria. Yet the tradition was modified at its very core, at the center from which its life sprang. In Greece art had developed as an expression of community life, social, political, and religious. In Rome it was prized as a foreign luxury, the privilege of pomp and power. The hundreds of statues from this period which fill our museums are for the most part cold and dull, only important for the history of sculpture as even poor illustrations are useful for a textbook on art. It is only in the portraits, in sculptured reliefs, in architectural monuments and sarcophagi, and in a few wall paintings that signs of genuine life may be found. Even here it is the subject rather than artistic excellence that claims attention. The simplicity of Greek relief gave way to an " illusionism " like that of painting, namely the tendency to representation of the photographic type, and here without the restraint and the design which raise a work of art out of the material into the spiritual world. The planes of relief were multiplied to stress the third dimension, masses of figures were often crowded into a limited space, or again very long bands of relief were used to develop a historical theme. Yet the types and devices of the Greek tradition still prevailed.

Nor was there any radical change when Christianity was recognized as the religion of the state. Hermes bearing a ram now becomes the Good Shepherd with a lamb; even scenes from

Greek mythology were shifted to tell a Christian story; the dove of Aphrodite was used to symbolize the Holy Spirit, the peacock, the bird of Hera, became the symbol of the resurrection, and the vine of Bacchic revel became the True Vine. This Graeco-Roman sculpture in the service of a new religion persisted through the welter of changes which followed the overthrow of Rome as a world power, even to the statues adorning early Romanesque churches in Provence, the last stage in the unbroken course of a tradition which had prevailed for a millennium and a half.

In the eastern Mediterranean world, meantime, new forces were at work. Much as Christianity owed to Greek thought, especially in the development of its theological dogma, it remained in essence an oriental religion of mysticism and other-worldliness. The Nicene creed is no Hellenic product. In particular the wonder of the human body, ever the delight of Greece, became anathema. In the Byzantine empire architecture developed in a manner quite foreign to the ideas of the west; in the eighth century sculpture of the human form came under the ban of idolatry; painting and mosaic and the decorative arts were handled from a point of view quite different from that of Greece. Mainly devoted to the service of religion, art made an appeal with dogmatic aim but essentially emotional and mystical, while the means it employed were intricate form and rich color. Great as was its debt to Greece in the way of types, technical processes, and formal devices, Byzantine art was imbued with a new spirit at variance equally with the clear untroubled vision of Greece and the practical genius of Rome.

Such was the art brought by merchants, as well as by pilgrims, wandering monks, and crusaders to western Mediterranean ports, or up the Danube and across country to western Europe. Illuminated manuscripts, carved wood and ivory enamels, wrought metal work, rich textiles, architectural sketches came first to Italy and eventually to monasteries and to the houses of feudal lords in the north. Welcomed as a church art, it was fostered in monasteries like Cluny, which became centers of inspiration for builder and decorator; and it found expression in the countless churches erected, especially in France, in the eleventh and twelfth centuries. But perhaps it was the Graeco-Roman tradition in southern France which led to the free use of the human figure, along with animals, birds, trees, and flowers, as sculptured decoration for architecture. From this beginning, in the region which was to become France, Gothic sculpture presently developed in local schools. Everywhere, though in varying degree, it is marked by a virile naturalism of pose, gesture, and feature. Everywhere the delight of the creator in his work is manifest, not so much the professional artist as the artisan who had learned the developing traditions of his craft. Much as the craft had learned from the east or from provincial Roman sculpture in southern France, its real kinship to the spirit of Greece lies in the fact that it is the outgrowth from roots planted deep in the economic, political, and religious life of the people. And it is totally at variance with Greek work in that it sought to express eternal spiritual values, as over against the values of daily human life. It is often didactic; it is emotional and full of the mysticism of the east; the source of its power is the controlling sense of the divine Personality in whom we live and move and have our being.

The Italian Renaissance marks the return to the Greek point of view, and in some measure to the Graeco-Roman tradition. While it was not primarily a revival of the sciences and arts and philosophy of ancient Greece, it was inevitable that science should build on the foundations which had been laid there, as these became known; that art and literature should be inspired by and to some degree follow models from a great, not alien, past; and that philosophy should profit by the works of such penetrating thinkers as the Greeks. Essentially the Renaissance was a rebirth of the higher human life, social, political, industrial, and economic, intellectual, and aesthetic. The fact that it began in Italy where the stream of classical influence had never disappeared, inevitably developed this dependence of the new life on the old. Though the Christian church had shifted the center of gravity in human life from the passing material world to a spiritual and eternal universe, the forms of Christian thought and practice were in large measure determined by its Greek heritage. With the demand for education universities were founded where classical learning and classical literature were expounded. In this newly awakened world classical tradition was controlling.

Specifically, the most fundamental feature of the Renaissance was the revival of humanism, of an absorbing interest in man and in the world in which he lived. In a sense this attitude toward man and his world was anti-Christian, a return to the early Greek point of view which conceived of life in terms of human needs and human satisfactions, though as in Greece these needs and satisfactions were often placed on a high plane. Inevitably humanism meant an interest in all classical remains, which fed the new spirit and gave form to its expression. And thus it came about that the Renaissance involved the rebirth of classical culture with its love for art and for literature.

The direct knowledge of ancient art was far more limited than the knowledge of classical literature. Yet Italy was filled with the ruins of Roman buildings, temples, market-places, theaters, triumphal arches, as well as aqueducts and bridges. Sculptured relief still remained on many of these structures. Sarcophagi remained from pre-Christian and early Christian times. Of the statues with which the cities had been so plentifully adorned, some still were known and occasionally others came to light in excavations for new buildings. Further, some examples of the minor arts still existed, utensils of metal and pottery and glass, as well as coins, medals, and engraved gems. From the fourteenth century on, the enthusiasm for the antique led to collections of Graeco-Roman art (such as the collection of engraved gems, coins, and reliefs gathered by Cosimo de' Medici in Florence, and the collections of sculpture made by the Popes, which found a permanent home when the Vatican Museum was established in 1770), till the artists, who arose to meet the demand of the new humanism for artistic expression, had opportunity to learn the classical tradition. Greek subjects, designs, and types, Greek technical processes and formal devices, the Greek principle of construction in design, became known to the new art in its infancy. As the biographer Vasari reports to us, Nicola d'Apulia, Andrea Pisano, Ghiberti, Donatello, Verrochio, and Michelangelo drew their inspiration from the remains of classical art. The Graeco-Roman tradition was reborn in the Italian Renaissance, a true rebirth in forms to meet the new age. The debt of the Renaissance art to Greece is incalculable.

Meantime in the north also the revival of political, economic, and intellectual life was attended by a " renaissance " of sculpture and painting only less important than the Renaissance in Italy. The distinctively northern painting seems to have begun with the miniature paintings of religious manuscripts, and to have developed along the lines suggested by illuminations, in the form of larger paintings for churches and monasteries. Apparently the illuminated manuscripts, often even those of Italian origin, were in the manner of the eastern church, a Greek tradition modified both by the influence of the Byzantine church and by other influences centering in the Byzantine world. Thus the beginners of painting in the north learned Greek methods, designs, and types mainly through the eastern church, rather than from the Graeco-Roman sculpture which had so much effect on the Italian Renaissance. And sculpture, also, while it had learned something from the carved relief of religious utensils, was guided in design, in its treatment of the human figure, and in its themes by scenes familiar in manuscript illuminations. Thus the eastern Greek tradition was present to guide the painting and sculpture which arose to meet the demands of the new age.

At a time when the church was no longer the unique center of learning or so controlling a force in the daily life of men, Gothic art lost much of its fresh power. In Flanders and Burgundy and presently in Germany the genius of the north developed a new art consonant with the newly awakened life of the age. It produced painting and sculpture to adorn both the homes of feudal lords and merchant princes and also the chapels and tombs with which these leaders enriched the churches. In its treatment of religious themes, in its portraits, in its presentation of themes from daily life, and in its landscapes, the new interest in man and his world marks the revival of humanism. This humanism, essentially akin to the Greek point of view, gave shape to two factors, the emotional mysticism and the realism of expression which were characteristic of the north. The debt of the northern Renaissance to Greece is not to be minimized.

IN THE centuries following the Renaissance the influence of the classical tradition has varied with the different arts. Just as in architecture it has always been a potent force, even when crowded into the background by other styles, so in modern sculpture it has been controlling in spite of occasional reactionary tendencies. In Italy the classical tradition in sculpture was so strong that, even after the achievements of the Renaissance, the very idea of sculpture was determined by the norm of classical remains. So persistent was this idea that it was not limited to Italy, and Rome, the home of these remains, became the one center of training and inspiration for sculptors. In the seventeenth century large collections of Greek and Roman sculpture were gathered in Italy. In 1623 the Ludovisi collection included 300 marbles. Although France became the great center of artistic production, her young students were trained in Italy even before the foundation of the French Academy in Rome in 1666; and the sculptors of Austria and Germany and the north were sent to Rome or to Paris for their training.

The result was that the late classical tradition in sculpture became dominant in Europe. Gothic sculpture and the early sculpture of the northern Renaissance disappeared as a creative force, their vitality sapped by the claims of Italian methods and Italian ideals. The baroque revolt of Bernini had little influence outside Italy, for it was classical remains which foreign artists came to Italy to study. The naturalism of a French sculptor like Pigalle, as well as the sentimental and often frivolous sculpture of the period of Louis XV, gave way to the controlling classical tradition; nor was the power of this tradition permanently affected in the eighteenth century by the vitality of Clodion and Houdon.

Toward the end of the eighteenth century new discoveries in Italy stimulated enthusiasm for the imitation of the antique. The first result was the so-called neo-classic school, headed by Canova and Thorwaldsen. The cold and lifeless products of this school eventually lost their hold on the public and French sculptors attempted to cut loose from the old tradition. In the nineteenth century the discoveries in Greek lands presented quite a new conception of Greek sculpture at its best, as contrasted with the copies and imitations and late Greek works which had previously been known. The apparent revolt from tradition in the French sculpture of the last half of the nineteenth century has been in a measure the result of these discoveries, a return to ancient Greek ideals which had been quite unknown to sculptors who were familiar only with the conventions and methods that had come down through Rome. It was original Greek art which Rodin

loved, and to which Despian was so much indebted. The different trends in sculpture today mean, not that the classical tradition is no
longer controlling, but only that it is not followed in a blind, mechanical way. Our present
conception of what sculpture is, of its significance, and of the means by which it attains its
ends, is still, it is evident, determined by the
achievements of ancient Greece.

In the history of painting the course of classical tradition is very different, primarily because no examples of monumental painting
remain from the great period in Greece, and
because practically no paintings even from the
Graeco-Roman period were known till two centuries ago. It was a Greek tradition from the
east, modified both by eastern Christianity and
by eastern ideals in art, which had governed
religious painting in Italy, from about the
sixth century on. This Greek tradition had
brought with it from the east the manner and
technique of painting, the types of its figures,
the formal devices it uses, and to a certain extent the Greek principle of construction. Out
of the early religious painting Renaissance
painting had grown; and nurtured by the new
life of the period and the absorbing interest both

in the present world and in a glorious past, it had come to rich fruition. While the achievements of the Italian Renaissance in sculpture did not greatly modify a tradition based on Graeco-Roman remains, its achievements in painting established a new tradition effective through the centuries that followed. It is necessary, however, to remember the different elements in the new tradition — its debt to the new life of Italy, its debt to the revived humanism of Greece, its debt to northern realism, and its original debt to what it had learned from Greece through Byzantium.

It is the task of the history of painting to record the influence of the Renaissance tradition on modern painting in Europe and America, as well as the new movements which from time to time have modified it. In every century if not in every generation there have been classicists, and there have been now realists, now romanticists, now sentimentalists, now students of the science of accurate representation, now explorers of the field of imagination. The significant fact, however, is that western painting has not cut loose from its Hellenic origin. Renaissance painting, the immediate source of inspiration for later developments of this art in

the western world, was the outgrowth of a rebirth of Greek humanism; its debt to Greece
is clear to every student of the period; and as
the result of its influence the student of Greek
art finds the stamp of Greece on our later painting in all its varying phases.

In the decorative arts Greek influence is far
less marked. Classical remains of utensils of
various kinds and of jewelry were few even in
Italy before the excavations of the last two
centuries; and classical furniture and textiles
and wall decorations were practically unknown.
It was only in certain limited fields that the
principles of Roman architectural ornament
could naturally be transferred to the products
of industry. On the other hand examples of
the minor arts had brought the eastern Greek
tradition to Italy and later to France, so that,
particularly in religious art, the influence of
Greece in this field was felt in the west. But
other factors were also present, such as textiles
purely eastern in design and workmanship, and
Saracenic metal work. Moreover native elements of design from the northern races persisted in household industries. And by the
seventeenth and eighteenth centuries Chinese
porcelain and lacquer work and small carvings

were brought to the European market, with the result that oriental design appeared at times in European furniture, in textiles, and particularly in European pottery and porcelains. That Greek ornament and Greek principles of design have nevertheless exerted considerable influence on western decorative arts since the

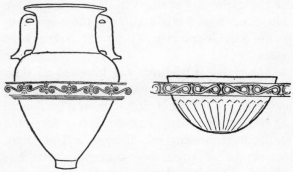

FIG. 5a. (left) BOEOTIAN POTTERY VASE
FIG. 5b. (right) GLASS BOWL FOR INDIRECT LIGHTING

Renaissance, gives evidence of the power of the classical tradition in this field. The maeander, the wave pattern, even the honeysuckle patterns, as well as spirals and rosettes, in the form inherited from Greece, have never disappeared from the decorative arts of the West. To mention but one example, the glass bowls

[73]

used for semi-indirect electric lighting today in a Boston hotel are moulded at the top with a band of running spirals having darts in the angles, a pattern which appears in almost the same form on a Boeotian vase with moulded decoration, to be found in the Boston Museum of Fine Arts (Fig. 5); while the lower part of the globe has vertical flutings, such as are found on a geometric vase in the same museum and frequently on Etruscan bucchero vases.

The classical tradition has imposed no slavish bondage on western painting, the minor arts, or sculpture. Rather, it has been a guide and an inspiration to later Europe; it has suggested paths by following which later artists might better realize their own conceptions; it has placed a wealth of material at the disposal of these artists — devices, types, and guiding principles for their efforts; and it has set standards by which later ages might judge their own work.

IV. THE SPIRIT OF GREEK ART

A FIRST examination of the classical tradition has yielded many details of style which succeeding ages owe to Greece. With all the fluctuations of this tradition, the revolts from it and the returns to it, and the foreign influences which at times gained dominance, the persistence of the tradition marks it as one controlling factor in the development of western art. Outwardly it is made up of types and forms and methods which have come down through Rome and Byzantium, and which have lost much of their original meaning. Much as these external forms do to make Greek art seem familiar to the modern world, the question remains whether it is possible to learn something about the spirit which found expression in these details; for it is the nature and significance of art as determined by the spirit of the Greek people which have controlled the course of western art. The creative power of Greece in the aesthetic as in the intellectual field was at its height for some three

centuries and then began to decline. Can we
discover in these creative centuries anything of
the source of that inspiration which left such
a heritage to the art of Europe? The details
of the classical tradition may be felt as fetters
in an age like the present. Our conception,
however, of what art is and what it means to
humanity, remains essentially what it was in
ancient Greece. The topic to be considered in
this chapter is the spirit of Greece and in particular the expression of it in art.

To give a definition of it in words is hardly
possible. We constantly speak of the spirit of
a city like Boston, or of a college like Yale, just
as we speak of the lawyer or merchant type of
mind. These we can describe, for the phrases
are not without meaning, but it would be idle
to attempt any adequate definition of them: all
one can do is to describe the type of mind and
the attitude toward life which they imply.
Similarly in speaking of the Greek spirit, what
we mean is the Greek attitude toward life, toward the world of nature and the human world,
and also the type of mind which led to this
attitude.

In the first place the physical world was a
reality for the Greeks. This conception was

[76]

not invalidated by philosophic speculation which sought to find one Being underlying the world of nature. The early Ionic philosophers found this Being in some one element like water or air or fire, the Pythagoreans found it in number, Plato and his followers in ideas. Yet the fact remains that natural science was born in Greece because the essential reality of the physical world was a fundamental conception of Greek thought, none the less clear and effective because some philosophers sought to penetrate behind it. The conception is in startling contrast to the Indian belief that matter is pure illusion, and essentially different from our modern idea of the world as a process of change which we call evolution. The effect of this attitude on art will be considered later; but it goes without saying that if things are conceived as real and the body of man is real, this consciousness lends a new meaning to representation in painting and sculpture.

But while the world of nature was a reality, it was interpreted in terms of the human spirit. The Greek was " at home in the world " because he felt it akin to himself. The restless sea was Poseidon, the grain-bearing earth was Demeter, the streams that rushed down from the hills were river-gods as the springs were nymphs. The life of forests and meadows was found in the nymphs who dwelt in them. The winds were beings of violent temper, enchained by Aeolus till he chose to let them loose. No greater contrast can be imagined than that between this conception of the world in terms of the human spirit, and the modern idea of the universe in terms of mechanical forces. Theirs was a human world, ours is an all but infinite machine in which the position of man is small indeed. It is almost inevitable that we should look on this Greek conception as purely poetic, a mere play of the imagination. Even granted that this is so, we must remember that such is not the Greek point of view. To the Greek the interpretation of the world in terms of his own spirit was not a fancy but a fact. It was the outgrowth of his experience, an empirical interpretation of life, which in turn shaped and vivified all his developing activities. Indeed the philosopher now might say that all our conceptions of force and the relation of forces are based on our bodily feelings of muscular activity overcoming resistance, and therefore that we too are interpreting the world in terms of a narrower activity of the human spirit; in other words that our procedure is the same as that of the Greeks, only more barren of spiritual values and because of its narrowness more useful in explaining the physical world. Our difficulty lies in the effort to realize the simplicity and directness of the Greek point of view. We are confused by the romantic current of thought, which not so long ago tempted writers and painters to depict a world of imagination in which one might find refuge from the barrenness as well as the hardships of a work-a-day world. The Greeks were not romanticists. It is part of Greek humanism to interpret the world in human terms, and humanism is at the very root of Greek art.

One result of the acceptance of the physical world as real and the interpretation of it in terms of man, was that for the Greeks the ideal was in experience, not outside it, and that it included all of experience. There have been civilizations in which the ideal, the effort for something higher and better than the satisfaction of momentary impulse or activity based on mere habit, seems to have played but little part. Today the goal of human effort seems to be the progressive mastery of the material world for the comfort and satisfaction of mankind — certainly an ideal in man's experience but not including all of experience, since there is scant place in it for purely intellectual, imaginative, and spiritual activities. The Nirvana, the ultimate goal of human effort in Indian philosophy, is as far outside the range of human experience as the heaven of our Middle Ages, that future world free from suffering and every evil for those who here have guided their lives to reach that goal. In contrast with such conceptions the Greek ideal was found within the world of everyday experience. The effort to make this world a better place for man had no large place in it, since the Greek lived for himself, for his family, and for his state. He was concerned only with what is and with the best there is. He sought to train his body to be as perfect as possible while he trained his mind to function as perfectly as might be in the world of his daily life. In this world his social instincts had free play, his sense for beauty full satisfaction, and his mind every stimulus to activity. Naturally this ideal of the perfect soul in the perfect body had a profound effect on the representative arts.

When one turns from the Greek attitude toward the external world to the Greek type

of mind, a real difficulty looms in his path.
The Greeks were not a simple homogeneous
folk. Their literature constantly dwells on
the differing types of different groups, pleasure-
loving Ionians and earnest Dorians, warlike
Spartans, commercial Corinthians, stolid Boeo-
tians and quick-witted Athenians, simple, pastoral Arcadians. But while the Greeks never
became one nation till these states yielded to
the military power of Macedon, there are certain marked characteristics, found in varying
degree in the different states, but distinct
enough to form a common type of mind.

Perhaps one may speak of an element of
restlessness in the Greek race. They are wan-
derers when they first appear on the stage of
history, migrating tribes slowly penetrating
down into the Balkan peninsular. No doubt
pressure from other migrating peoples started
the movement by causing a shortage of pasture-
lands and hunting fields; it is fair to assume not
that the Greeks wanted to move, but rather
that they were ready to go and did go, when
less venturesome tribes stayed behind. The
second millennium B.C. apparently was marked
by successive waves of migration, until the
Greek race occupied their future home, and

overflowed across the Aegean. And in later days the Greeks seem to have been travellers, gradually dispossessing the Phoenicians in their control of commerce by sea, but also travellers for the sake of seeing new lands and new peoples. That the *Iliad,* with its theme of glorious war beyond the sea, should have been composed at all and should have been a constant source of entertainment for so many centuries; that the *Odyssey,* with its tales of adventurous voyages and strange lands and strange peoples, should have been linked with the *Iliad* as a main feature of the bard's repertory in every Greek land, is witness if witness were needed to the spirit of the wanderer and the traveller in those who listened to them. The contrast between these Greeks and their neighbors may justify us in calling them restless.

Certainly they were restless-minded, alert, curious, interested to see or to hear some new thing. Out of curiosity about the natural world science was born; for centuries this mental trait inspired the effort of philosophy to understand both the world and man; it was a force impelling men to explore new fields in literature and music and sculpture and painting as well as in the practical arts.) Yet the Greeks as a race were not fickle, because of their clear vision for what was good and the tenacity with which they held on to each new achievement when once it met their approval. The " Works and Days " of Hesiod, that mass of practical and curious lore, is an early example of the investigating mind in the natural world. But it is in the drama that one sees at its best this eagerness to know the world here, the human world in all its rich values; for all of Athens shared with enthusiasm the dramatist's study of man's passions and failures and successes, of the fate which he could not escape but which he could meet with courage. In philosophy the contrast with India is striking. Indian philosophy is the product of introspection and meditation, while Greek thinkers were alive to every new experience in their effort to understand the world, its significance and its values. In fact every phase of mental activity was an adventure, eagerly pursued by this restless-minded people.

Men have often asked what would have been the result for the world if the Persians had been victorious at Salamis and Plataea, and if Greece proper had thus been made a province of the Persian empire; for Persia was a highly organized military empire with small place for individual initiative or for the growth of the higher arts of civilization. The Greeks, on the contrary, were a high-spirited people, ever inspired by their love of freedom. Freedom did not mean for them license, nor did it mean individualism in our sense of the term, that is, a keen sense of value of the individual, and of his rights and his duties. The individual belonged to the family, the tribe, and the state, of which he was but one unit. Freedom did mean the right to self-development and self-satisfaction as one member of a society in which laws were enacted, taxes imposed, public works constructed, and order maintained with the consent of the governed. It was only a member of the old aristocracy of Athens who would describe democracy as the rule of the tyrant Demos. This love of freedom for the individual in the state was at Athens a constant stimulus to thought and to the expression of thought in literature and art. Further, pride in a free state like Athens led to the erection of public buildings and statues for which the most talented artists of the world were in demand.

Directness and clarity were marked traits

[84]

of the Greek mind. To face with clear vision the world, particularly the human world, to grasp what is essential and overlook the accidental, to coördinate the results in a reasoned system, such was the natural procedure of this gifted folk. The peculiarity of Greek thought as compared with modern thought, was its tendency to use concrete terms. While a scientific age like the present revels in abstractions, it was the Greek method to express thoughts, ideals, and human values so far as possible concretely. Perhaps it was for this reason that geometry made greater progress in Greece than other branches of mathematics, for its generalizations could be expressed in concrete figures. The tendency affects even language. Where we say with dry accuracy " The running of the horse is graceful," it would be natural for the Greek to say " The horse runs gracefully." This bent for the concrete might have led to absorption in details, and it would not encourage the abstract sciences, but it formed the most favorable soil for the growth of the drama and of such arts as sculpture and painting. Such characters as Prometheus and Antigone and Medea, such sculpture as the Apollo pediment at Olympia,

[85]

the Hermes of Praxiteles, the Aphrodite from Melos, are the result of Greek clarity and directness of thought as applied to human experience. And it is this element of the universal expressed in concrete form, which lends to Greek literature and art their power to touch every succeeding age.

It remains to speak more particularly of the method of coördination and systematization which was natural to the Greek mind. In dealing with the concrete facts of experience, material or spiritual, it was governed by a keen sense of order and harmony. In truth its method was aesthetic rather than mystical or coldly logical. In Greek thought about ethical problems this principle is very evident. While other peoples have found a rule of life in detailed commandments of God as did the ancient Hebrews, or in a reasoned logical system like that of Calvin or of Kant, or in the means for reaching some distant goal like the mediaeval Christian heaven, the Greeks defined the good life in terms of order and harmony in the spirit of man. Central among the virtues was moderation or temperateness ($\sigma\omega\phi\rho\sigma\sigma\acute{\nu}\nu\eta$), the embodiment of the principle " nothing in excess " ($\mu\eta\delta\grave{\epsilon}\nu$ $\mathring{\alpha}\gamma\alpha\nu$) which guided all ethical

[86]

thought. The main source of evil in the soul was insolence or overweening pride (ὕβρις), which led Ajax to destruction when he defied Poseidon, and which involved Oedipus in patricide and incest with all the suffering that followed in their train. When Aristotle analyzes the different virtues, he finds each a mean between two extremes, as courage is a mean between fear and rashness, using the aesthetic principle of ordered balance to explain each virtue. This was a system of ethics based immediately on the experiences of life without recourse to any external basis of right and wrong; and the facts of daily life were coördinated and interpreted by the sense for order and harmony. It is almost true to say that for the Greeks the good soul was the beautiful soul.

In the Greek theory of the state the same principle of balanced forces and harmonious order was a determining factor. It was not usual for the Greeks to speak of the state as an organism, its different activities combined in one whole as in a biological organism, yet their thought of the state would almost suggest this overworked metaphor. Certainly the play of living forces balanced in a harmonious whole underlies Greek thought of the state. In other words the principle governing their idea of the good state was the same as that governing their idea of the good man, in that the facts of political experience were coördinated by the sense for order and harmony.

Much the same may be said about Greek study of the physical world. Data as to the heavenly bodies came to Greece from Egypt if not from Mesopotamia, and observation added greatly to these data. The facts were combined and interpreted variously, but always from an aesthetic point of view, in a " beautiful " system. Aristotle recognizes this when in a striking passage he speaks of Nature's purposes and deep-seated laws " all tending in her multitudinous work to one form or another of the Beautiful." [1] The Pythagorean conception of the music of the spheres was no mere metaphor; rather it was a serious attempt to explain astronomical facts by a theory based on the sense of harmony. \In biology the alert minds of the Greeks gathered an enormous mass of accurate

[1] Τὸ γὰρ μὴ τυχόντως ἀλλ' ἕνεκά τινος ἐν τοῖς τῆς φύσεως ἔργοις ἐστὶ καὶ μάλιστα· οὗ δ'ἕνεκα συνέστηκεν ἢ γέγονε τέλους, τὴν τοῦ καλοῦ χώραν εἴληφεν. Arist., De part. Anim., I. 5; 645ᵃ 23. The English translation is from D'Arcy W. Thompson, On Aristotle as a Biologist, Oxford, 1913, p. 16.

information; their descriptions of species, and their accounts of habitats and life-habits of animals and plants are not without value today; but here again the various principles of classification suggested were aesthetic rather than strictly logical. It was Alcmaeon, a pupil of Pythagoras, who extended his researches into the field of physiology and medicine, laying down the principle that health depends on the harmony, disease on the discord of the elements which go to make up the body. A century or more later Hippocrates, who laid the foundation for the science of medicine, made this aesthetic theory more explicit. He held that health depends on the harmonious distribution of the four elements and the four cardinal fluids in the body, so that disease was to be cured by restoring the disturbed harmony in the relation of these elements and humors. Thus the beginnings of science in Greece, sound and important as they were, consisted first in the accurate observation of concrete facts, and secondly in a systematization of these facts by using the same aesthetic principle of order and harmony which governed the thought of man and the state.

[89]

IT WOULD be rash indeed to study the mental traits of a people as a basis for predicting the nature of their art, or even for learning whether they developed any real art. At the same time it is clear that the Greek mind was marked by traits which suggest art as a natural means of expression. Their sense for reality, their poetic interpretation of the material world in human terms, their effort to realize an ideal in experience, the directness and concreteness of their thought, in particular their use of harmony and rhythm as the principle for coördination in their study of the soul, of society, and of the physical world, all point to a type of mind which naturally would work on aesthetic lines. But the problem is not whether to expect a high development of art in Greece. Rather it is to understand what we can of an art which has been the rich heritage of the western world for these two millenniums. The very nature of Greek art, its moving spirit rather than its outward forms, is the real legacy of Greece to later civilization; and this can only be understood by first studying the mind that created it.

* * *

I

PERHAPS the first characteristic of Greek art to strike the modern student is its communal character. Of course there are schools of art today, rapidly changing schools, but the artist works as an individual; he seeks self-expression; his aim is to be original. He paints what he sees or what he feels; then he seeks approval for his personal achievement. In art as in other phases of human activity, the dependence of the individual on the community tends to be forgotten. The Greeks stressed the value of the community which gave to the individual the sphere of activity in which he might find freedom, scope for all his talents, and the stimulus to realize his ideals. The Greek artist worked as a member of the community, trained in the legacy of its past, inspired by its sympathetic appreciation, seeking to express more and more perfectly its ideals. His statue or painting was successful, not when he expressed himself, but when he expressed the life of the group.

It may seem strange that we know so little of the men who made the Parthenon sculptures. We know only that Pheidias was re-

sponsible for the work. It goes without saying
that the completion of so great a task demanded
a considerable number of artisans trained to
work together in the manner prescribed for
them. The Parthenon frieze is one work of
art, but a comparison of adjacent figures often
shows slight differences in technique, which
indicate that they were not cut by the same
person. Payments to the sculptors of the
Erechtheum frieze are recorded in extant in-
scriptions, sixty drachmas a figure to each of
various workmen. A recent analysis [1] of the
Nike bastion frieze discriminates the technical
methods of four different stone-cutters. Yet
in each instance the result was a unified whole,
a group-product which was a single work of
art. Again, vase paintings of the best period
are often inscribed with the name of potter
and painter, " Makron was the maker," " Hi-
eron was the painter "; but the name of the
potter means only the small shop where a few
workmen made vases for the master with
whose name they were labelled, if indeed the
name of the painter means more than that the
drawing was done in his style and under his

[1] Cf. Rhys Carpenter, in *American Journal of Archaeology*, XXXIII. 467–483 (1929).

direction. These simple objects also were produced by groups of artisans whose talent justifies us in calling them artists.

Further, the themes of painting and sculpture were chosen for their appeal to the community. When the enthusiasm of the people was focussed on an athlete, victorious in pan-Hellenic games, it found expression in a statue erected in some public place, not a portrait statue of the individual but a figure like Myron's Discobolus (Plate XIII*a*), suggesting the typical athlete. Harmodius and Aristogeiton (Plate XI*a*), champions of the people against enslaving tyrants, were honored by a statue representing their attack on entrenched power. Statues of the gods in temples or public places gave visual form to Greek thought of these gods, to Zeus the divine ruler in his pan-Hellenic shrine at Olympia, to Hera the queen at Argos, or to such a god as Dionysus, the power which inspired the poet and embodied the spirit of life in vegetation. These statues were not so much the creation of one sculptor or another; rather, it was the artist's function to make visible the beings which the imagination of the community had created through generations of reflection. Similarly the decorative

[93]

sculpture on temples and mural paintings in halls and porticos represented myths of heroes, which were the deposit of imaginative thought during the long past. These legends, consecrated by age, are simply interpreted by the artist to serve his purpose. Even when, toward the end of the fifth century, sculptors began to make portraits, the aim was not so much to produce an exact likeness as to give concrete form to the impression which a Sophocles or a Demosthenes had made on the community.

Moreover, it was for the public that painting and sculpture were produced. Private collectors were unknown before Roman times. A man might have a beautifully cut stone to serve as his personal seal, or a vase painted by some noted artist, or a graceful piece of furniture in his house for his own enjoyment. Statues, however, were erected in the palaestra or in the agora or in a temple court, and paintings decorated the walls of public halls. They belonged to the community out of which sprang the subject they depicted, from which the artist drew his inspiration, and for which he sought to embody his vision. For the visual arts, no less than poetry and the drama, depended on the public. It was only a people which found its highest satisfaction in great tragedy, that could produce an Aeschylus or a Sophocles; only a people with keen appreciation of perfect form as a means of expression, for whom Pheidias could create his Zeus or Praxiteles his Cnidian Aphrodite.

II

SECONDLY, the spirit of Greek art was progressive. In contrast with the sculpture of Assyria and Egypt, Greek sculpture in every period shows the alert, investigating mind of the race. In Egypt the finest sculpture belongs to the Fourth Dynasty, the period of the great pyramids; we know little of how it developed, but at this date the types were already fixed for seated and standing figures both in the round and in relief; for three millenniums these types persisted with little substantive change, certainly with no progress in conception or workmanship. And if we turn to the art of the east, we find that it changes with different phases of civilization, but always within certain conventions; sensitive as it is to life and thought, it can hardly be called progressive. Possibly because of changes in Greek civilization, which rose to a rapid climax in the sixth and fifth centuries B.C., the course of Greek art is a steady progress. Decade by decade one may trace the effort of the sculptor to reach a more perfect result; experiments are tried, then modified or discarded; marble is found superior to limestone, and color is subordinated to texture; first simpler forms of the body are mastered, then the more complex; the pose and rhythm of the figure are better understood. Not that there is any effort for novelty as such, at least before Hellenistic times; but the artist is consistently seeking some truer, deeper, finer expression of his subject. Vagaries are avoided or checked because art is an affair of the group, for which the artist is only the spokesman, and the life of the group is rooted in a sound tradition.

The venturesome spirit of the early sculptor is shown in primitive pediment sculpture found on the Athenian acropolis. In the Typhon group he took the old " Apollo " type, cut off from the waist down (UPA, pl. 41).[1] Three such figures side by side at different angles formed the front part of the monster, while, with no attempt at transition, the twisted tail runs off into the corner of the pediment. The

[1] UPA, *i.e.*, University Prints, Series A, Boston, 1916.

[96]

crouching Heracles wrestling with the Triton
(Plate VIII*a*) is a still bolder attempt to depict
a difficult subject. It was another school of
sculptors which perhaps half a century later
cut the figures of the Aegina temple; here the
wounded warrior (Plate VIII*b*) shows amazing progress in the knowledge of the figure in a
twisted position, while the face is crudely conceived. Another half century and the so-called
" Theseus " of the Parthenon pediment illus-
trates the solution of this problem (Plate VIII*c*)
— the problem of the reclining figure with
somewhat twisted torso — toward which for a
century or more the artist had made consistent
progress.

Perhaps it is in technical skill that this progress is most easily traced. The sculptor is
learning to know his materials and his tools.
A statue like the " Apollo " of Orchomenos
(Plate IX*a*) [1] shows indications of the method
practised in Egypt, where the outline of the figure was drawn on a thick rectangular block,
then the stone was cut back on these lines so
as to give a very thick representation of the
outline, after which the corners were cut off and
rounded to suggest the figure in the round. The

[1] Cf. also the female figure from Delos, UPA, pl. 20.

muscles are just bulges in the surface, lines are used to mark the groin, the eyes and mouth are hardly more than drawn with lines, and the mass of the hair is marked off by lines. The Hermes bearing the calf (Plate IX*b*) shows the same use of grooves and lines, and much the same bulges for muscles, along with marvellous progress in the power of the artist to express what he sees through the medium of stone. The gain in technical skill may be followed step by step in the Aegina marbles, the Olympia pediment figure, and the sculpture of the Parthenon, till in the work of Praxiteles the marble seems to be entirely plastic under his hand.

Closely allied with progress in technique is progress in vision and understanding of the subject. The early sculpture is like the drawings of a child who puts down what attracts his attention — a face must have eyes and mouth, whatever their relation, whether or not there is a nose. Even such advanced figures as most of the draped women found on the Athenian acropolis (e.g. Plate IX*c*) are made on the basis that a woman must have a carefully arranged garment, the breasts must be indicated, and, if the garment is drawn close, the hips; while the face has chin, mouth, nose, eyes, and

protruding cheek-bones, with little relation between them. In earlier male figures, the emphasis on detail is even more marked, as in the
knees and feet of the Tenea Apollo (Plate I),
while torso and face are treated in broad masses
with no proper transition to bring them together. But the artist's vision gradually comes
to grasp the whole as including details, while
the details themselves are better understood,
till a very simple handling of the subject, as in
the Parthenon frieze, suffices to express the
broader, deeper understanding which he has
gained.

And with progress in technique and design
comes progress in truth of representation. The
early sculptor devised various ornamental
methods for suggesting the hair of men and
women, all decorative, all looking like wigs
rather than like hair, and it was not till the
middle of the fifth century B.C. that the artist
could convey the impression of real hair. The
archaic smile (UPA, pl. 12), the over-developed
chest (UPA, pl. 15), the depression which fol-
lows the line of the midriff and extends below to
the bottom of the abdomen (UPA, pl. 57, 81),
and the sharp lines at the groin separating the
upper leg from the abdomen (UPA, pl. 15) are

not representation; rather the artist has supplied devices to give character to his figure when vision failed him. Yet decade by decade he learns to see his subject and to reproduce it, with detail subordinated to an organic whole. While the Aegina pediment sculptors gloried in their power to depict muscles (UPA, pl. 79–81), figures in the Olympia pediment (Plate XI*b*) show quite as much knowledge of anatomy but subordinated to a truer representation of the whole. But mere truth of outward form was never the sculptor's primary aim. The purpose of early design was doubtless to make the figures more alive; not simply in the relief but in the round the living being was the artist's theme, a result he sought first by suggesting motion as in the Harmodius and Aristogeiton (Plate XI*a*) and in Myron's Discobolus (Plate XIII*a*), then by the perfect rhythm of the Doryphorus (Plate X*a*) and the Lemnian Athena (Plate III).

Finally, progress in effective design kept step with other gains in the sculptor's power. Not only were the early figures meant to be seen from only one point of view, the direct front view, but the design of the artist was primarily linear, as if the figure were a drawing to which thickness or depth had been added in a somewhat mechanical way. The rippling ribs of the Strangford Apollo (Plate X*b*), the divisions of the torso by horizontal and vertical lines, for example in the Ligourio bronze (Plate X*c*) and in the figure of Aristogeiton (Plate XI*a*), and the use of lines to define the muscles in the Lancelotti Discobolus (Plate XIII*a*) show how this linear design was brought into harmony with representation. But very early comes the beginning of design in planes, the three-dimensional design which differentiates sculpture from drawing and painting. It has made progress by the time of the Aristogeiton, it comes to its own in the work of Pheidias and Polycleitus, and in the use of subtle transitions to produce simple, appealing effects it reached a level unknown before or since in the work of Praxiteles.

Progress in these different directions can only be understood by remembering the intensity of life, which sought expression in the sixth and fifth centuries B.C. and by keeping in mind the communal nature of Greek art. Only in an atmosphere of constant stimulus and criticism could the eager, open mind of the sculptor make such consistent gain toward his goal. Rooted in the distant past, nurtured by intelligent appreciation, this art grew steadily till it produced the rich fruit which was its destiny.

III

THIRDLY, the humanism of the Greeks profoundly affected their art. This humanism meant that their primary interest was in man and in what differentiates man from the rest of the world, that is, his ideas, his purposes, his relations with his fellowmen, the human values he found in life. The effect of this on art was first that the main theme of painting and sculpture and even of the decorative arts was the human form, and secondly that the Greek interpretation of the world and of life was expressed by art in personalities that were both divine and human. It is true that from earliest times representative art has been quite generally devoted to the human figure. Our interest in still life and landscape is mainly a modern affair, for, apart from abstract design, in earlier ages it was the mystery of life, particularly human life, which attracted the artist and his public. Nevertheless, the purpose and the procedure of the Greek artist was essentially different from that of his predecessors, so different that it changed the course of later art in Europe. Finding the human form a very complex subject, subtly varied in its planes, not to mention the variations due to changing mental states, the predecessors of the Greeks practically gave up the attempt to reproduce it truthfully in sculpture and painting; instead of utilizing the skill they gained for an increasingly truer treatment of their subject, they were satisfied with working out a general formula for the purpose. The conventional types developed, for example, in Egypt and Assyria, different as they are, are each wonderfully effective in what they attempt to do; but because men are presented in studied conventions, a relief like the Assyrian wounded lioness in the British Museum, and certain Egyptian paintings of birds and animals, seem to us to have far more life and reality than scenes from human life. The Greek artist, in contrast with his predecessors, was not daunted by the difficulty of his subject. Avoiding conventions, however clever, he consistently made it his aim to present the human form in painting and sculpture as truthfully and vividly as he could, and every increase in technical skill and in

[103]

vision meant progress toward this goal. It was the goal of humanism.

The very function of art in Greece was on a different plane from that of earlier art. It was not a product of the " play-impulse," however keenly the artist may have enjoyed his task; it had no mystical or magical purpose, like control through the image he made over an enemy or over the game he hunted. Nor was it a record art. Skillful conventions sufficed for the record of royal achievements in Egypt and Assyria, as they sufficed to secure safety for the soul after death in Egypt and divine favor for the living ruler in Assyria. It was in Greece for the first time that man as such was the theme of art.[1] And the reason was the Greek conception of man. From the Greek point of view the living body was the man himself. Just as life was there, though it could only be seen as animating the body, so the thinking, feeling, purposeful spirit was there, and it too could be seen as the body yielded its energy to the thinking mind, or expressed emotion, or carried out some high purpose of the man him-

[1] The beginning of this interest in man and his activities, such as war, hunting, and athletic games, is found in Minoan and Mycenaean art.

[104]

self.   The Athenians could. *see* Pericles sway-
ing the assembly by his oratory, Pheidias making some statue of a god, a musician charming
them by his music, just as they saw their
compatriot winning in the Olympic games.
Granted that they saw not only life but the
human spirit in man's body, it was a logical
conclusion that the perfect spirit was to be
found in the perfect body; or, conversely, that
the theme of art, the perfect body, should be
and was the true expression of the highest development of the human spirit.   Moreover, the
habit of constant athletic exercise without garments gave artist and public an acquaintance
with the body, not simply the head, such as no
other civilized race has possessed.   When all
of life was ordered on the principle that body
and spirit should be developed to the highest
degree of perfection, a perfection visible in the
body, humanism gave the artist the greatest
opportunity he has ever had to treat man as his
subject.

The nature of humanism in Greek art becomes perhaps clearer when contrasted with
the humanism of mediaeval art in Europe.
Many of the figures of saints and attendants
in late Romanesque and early Gothic art are

very human in their expression of emotions such as love, pity, hope, surprise, and joy. These emotions are expressed by attitude and gesture [1] and by facial expression; but the body itself is covered and often hardly exists under the garments. To us, accustomed to see only gestures and the mobile face, these figures are very human and very much alive. Moreover, because they are individualized by their emotion, in contrast with the more universalized Greek types, they seem much nearer to us. But the mediaeval artist never depicted the whole man, body and mind as well as soul, nor was he interested in the perfection of man as was the Greek painter and sculptor. His one occupation was with the soul which only temporarily tenanted the body.

Humanism shows its controlling influence on Greek art not only in the principle that art deals primarily with man, but also in the conception of each subject which it presents. In a sense the interpretation of the world in human terms was a form of science, and its influence on art was only secondary. Of the count-

[1] Greek vases show that their painters knew well the value of attitude and gesture to express emotion, when these artists renounced the opportunities of sculpture and elaborated painting for this simple decorative work.

less forms with which the Greeks peopled the
sea — Oceanus, Nereus and the Nereids, Am-
phitrite, Ino and Leucothea, Glaucus, Triton,
etc., as well as Poseidon — and the land —
Gaia, nymphs of woodland and meadows and
springs, River gods, Pans and Satyrs, Seileni
and Maenads — very few appear in sculpture.
In painting the scope was wider, though it was
only on painted vases that the draughtsman
gave free scope to his skill in representing these
human spirits of nature. But who could doubt
that the sun and moon were charioteers of the
sky, when he saw Helios driving his horses out
of the sea at dawn, and Selene leaving the
heavens, on the east pediment of the Parthenon? And when a nymph like Cyrene became
the goddess of the city of that name, or Are-
thusa the patron of Syracuse, coins made their
heads familiar to the Greek world. Still, the
number of spirits whose personality was so
crystallized as to be deemed worthy of the
sculptor's attention was comparatively limited.

The effect of humanism on art is most evident in the statues of the gods. In earlier civilizations gods were sometimes given an animal
form, like Aaron's golden calf, or a human
form with animal head, as often in Egypt, or

the form of men with some symbol to mark them as gods, as in Assyrian and Minoan art. In Greece the gods were not only given a human form, but for the first time in art they were given a human personality on a higher plane, and so distinctive that it was quite unnecessary to add any symbol to the statue. When a serpent is put with the statue of Athena at Athens, it is to associate the cult of Erichthonius on the Acropolis with that of Athena, not to define the goddess; a dolphin with Poseidon marks the presence of the sea; and the stag with Artemis is the companion of the goddess. Commonly, however, even such symbols were not present, and the artist limits himself to showing the personality of the god. If in our copies we cannot always distinguish Asclepius from Zeus or Demeter from Hera, we are quite justified in blaming the copyist. In the great statue of Zeus by Pheidias no thunderbolt was necessary: the visitor to Olympia saw the " father of gods and men," the divine ruler of the universe who represents power and wisdom and justice tempered with mercy, the god in whom Greek religion made its nearest approach to monotheism. In the Demeter of Cnidos (Plate XIV*b*) we see the mother

[108]

mourning for her lost daughter, but not without the hint that Persephone has gone to the realm of souls whence she will return with the sprouting grain; for it is this same Demeter whose constant gift to mankind is the grain. In the person of Demeter it is the artist's task to present at least three phases of human experience, mother-love, love that death does not conquer, and the beneficence to which man owes the grain. Hermes is often shown with little wings on his feet or with the caduceus. But Hermes, too, is known by his human character, the divine messenger, god of travel and trade, the god who guided souls to the realm of Hades, and at the same time the patron of athletics. Though the statue by Praxiteles depicts him in a mood of relaxation, no one questions that it is a Hermes. While Athena is ordinarily shown with helmet and aegis, and shield and spear, she is no mere impersonation of war. Her practical wisdom which brought success to bold general and shrewd politician, was equally the source of women's skill in the arts of the home. In Athens she came to represent the spirit of that city; the embodiment of all that made Athens great. The so-called Lemnian Athena (Plate III) is no less Athena because she wears no helmet and her aegis is scarcely more than an ornament. The Artemis from Gabii (Plate XII*a*) is a different phase of the goddess from the Artemis of Versailles (Plate XII*b*), but she is the same person; for this complex being [1] is at the same time the goddess who protects wild life, and the patroness of hunters, and withal she is the goddess of childbirth for man and beast. Apollo, whose shafts deal destruction to his enemies, who at Delphi both foretells the future and points out the way of escape from devastating plague, the leader of the Muses and the god of music, Apollo is one person, whose nature the sculptor must depict in his image. It is the crowning achievement of humanism in Greek art to create these statues of the gods, divine beings made visible to their worshippers not only in their physical human form, but with the mind and individual personality of men.

In Roman days the influence of humanism was less strong, for the Roman gods were in themselves personified functions rather than persons. Juno was the wife, Ceres the giver of grain, Mercury the messenger, up to the time

---

[1] Cf. A. Fairbanks, *Handbook of Greek Religion, Appendix* I, New York, 1910.

when the Romans borrowed myth and literature and art from the Greeks. And early
Christian art represented prophets and apostles
and saints rather as types with their symbols
than as persons. It was not till the revival of
humanism with the Renaissance that the Greek
effort to depict personalities became again, as it
has remained in later Europe, the principle of
art in dealing with man.

IV

FOURTHLY, Greek art aimed at representation.
Lysippus, we are told, claimed that Nature was
his teacher. Plato regularly speaks of art as
mimetic, the imitation of the object by drawing
or painting or sculpture, on which ground he
condemns it in the *Republic* as a step away
from reality. To paint grapes so perfectly that
birds would try to peck them, or bees with such
detail that an observer might fear they would
sting him, or to make a bronze cow so real that
it would attract bulls, such was the ideal described by the Greek rhetoricians.

No such ideal guided the conventionalized
art of Mesopotamia and Egypt, to which reference has been made (p. 103). Their painting
and sculpture did not seek to present objects

[111]

as the eye sees them, but was satisfied with a
formula which had been developed to serve
the artist's purpose. Even the desire in Egypt
for sculptured portraits to serve as a body for
the wandering soul after death, led only to
modifications of the formula in the face which
was treated with discernment and sensitive feeling. Nor was it the case with the design art
of primitive peoples and early civilizations generally. Their art was essentially decorative.
It often consisted of abstract designs, and when
pictorial elements were introduced into the design, there was little or no effort for accurate
representation. The animals so truthfully
painted by the cave-dwellers of the Dordogne
are almost a unique exception to the rule, a
rule which is well exemplified by the grotesque
figures of early Central American art (p. 5 f.).
The art of Minoan civilization is of this decorative type. At its best it reproduces plant and
marine and human subjects with a wonderful
feeling for truth and beauty; nevertheless accuracy of representation was never the primary
aim of the Minoan artist. Certainly it was not
the aim of the symbolic art of India, where
subtle meaning quite takes the place of any
effort to reproduce the exact forms of nature.

Nor is the Chinese or Japanese painter concerned with forms as the eye sees them, when in a landscape he reproduces the feeling of high mountains and dashing streams and gnarled trees and misty distances; or when, like Sessiu, he paints not detailed forms of monkeys, but the life of monkeys as they sport over the trees; or again when he seeks to draw a bamboo branch in such a way that the observer would feel the wind bending and rustling it. On the contrary, the first point which impresses a student when he begins the study of Greek sculpture is inevitably the progress toward accurate representation. It belongs to the realm of scientific fact with which he is familiar. Whether or not he eventually comes under the spell of the objects he is studying and yields to their charm, he begins with the true observation that the method of Greek art is the representation of the object as seen.

Representation has been the keynote of western art now for centuries, till at last the " modernists " have revolted. Certainly in America we tend to think of art first as representation, plus all the complex of suggestion and emotion that goes with the subject. A picture is a picture of something, or people do not stop to look at it. We are inclined to classify paintings by their subjects, as portraits, land-scapes, *genre* scenes, etc.; and our public makes its first judgment of a picture by its success in presenting its subject. In fact the history of the development of art in Europe, particularly since the Renaissance, might be written as a history of modes of representation. Such is the controlling influence of the conception of art which was developed in Greece and passed on to later Europe.

This effort for accurate representation or imitation, as the Greeks called it, might suggest an art of realism. Realism is one of those tricky words which have acquired very differ-ent shades of meaning. As applied to art, it may mean an interest in rich detail, copied with loving care, as in Ruskin's drawings of leaves or architectural carvings. Neither Greek sculp-ture nor drawings on Greek vases nor the wall-paintings which survive from the Graeco-Roman period can be called realistic in this sense. It may mean a study of the objective facts of nature and the attempt to reproduce them with photographic accuracy, that is, with-out selection or organization. Greek representation is not of this type. And often the word is used to describe poetry and painting which deliberately choose subjects from the commonplace, perhaps sordid phases of daily life, and reproduce them with no reference to their possible significance but simply as facts. Such is not the Greek way. But if realism means directness and definiteness in art, if it means a simple effort to represent the object as the eye of the artist sees it, the word is rightly applied to Greek art. It was the function of this art to lay hold of and vividly express reality as a factor in human experience. In this sense also Greek art is rightly termed realistic, the forerunner of all that is worth while in the realistic art of later Europe.

At the same time this representation is idealistic. High ideals and noble style lift it out of the sphere of ordinary life, even though its aim is always to reproduce an ideal in human experience, in contrast with the idealism which finds its meaning outside the object itself or even outside human experience. The object is represented as the eye sees it, only as finer and more perfect, the finer and more perfect expression of its own nature. There was no

[115]

yearning for the unattainable, no effort to go beyond the Greek ideal of the perfect man. It is the idealization of human life.

The Greek gods are represented as distant from the world of man's trivial passions and activities; one can never forget that they are gods; yet they have not only a human form and a human personality, but their whole significance lies in the universal human experiences they idealize. The stories of Heracles and Theseus, of Lapiths and Centaurs, of the Amazons and of the Trojan war, as they appear on Greek temples, are presented with life and reality like a drama unfolding itself before the eyes of the spectator; at the same time the world in which the actors move is an idealized human world. Such an athletic figure as the Apoxyomenos (UPA, pl. 235) is both a most carefully studied presentation of the male form, and at the same time a figure idealized by the omission of everything that is accidental or that is so individualized as to interfere with the sculptor's theme. Even a portrait aims to be a true representation of the subject which his contemporaries saw, but all the truer because it expresses more of the man's own nature. The portraits of Sophocles and Demosthenes can hardly be classed with portraits " from life," for they are idealized figures like the portraits of Homer in a later period. To lift the subject out of the sphere of the commonplace but not out of the range of human experience, to depict it not as it may be seen casually but as the trained eye of the artist sees its true nature, such is Greek idealism in representation.

Writers on Greek sculpture often speak of its serenity, especially in works from the fifth century B.C. The meaning of this serenity is found in the idealism now under discussion, an idealism which places its subject in a world free from disturbing accident, its human aims raised to a higher plane, its very suffering a purifying force. Even such a representation of conflict as of the Lapiths and Centaurs on the Olympia pediment, leaves an impression of serenity for it is dominated by the controlling arm of Apollo. The Cresilas portrait of Pericles (Plate XIV*a*) is serene, for even in our copies it emphasizes the Olympian quality of the statesman. A grave relief like that set up to Hegeso (Plate XV*a*), which represents her taking a jewel from the casket her maid brings, barely hints at the sadness of death; it so em-

phasizes the beauty of the woman in her life
that it, like other monuments of its class,
breathes an atmosphere of serene idealism.

Closely allied with serenity is the restraint
and simplicity of Greek sculpture in the three
great centuries. The stele of Aristion (Plate
XIc) seems at first sight hardly more than a
drawing on stone, yet the low relief is so man-
aged as to give a clear impression of depth.
Every unnecessary detail is omitted; the surfaces of the face, the neck, the forearm and
hand, and the upper leg are handled with extreme simplicity; none the less the feeling of
the living body is there. The Delphi charioteer
(Plate XIIIb) is a striking example of Greek
restraint. The modelling of the face and arms
is in broad simple planes; the treatment of the
garment with its columnar folds is very simple;
only in the feet has the sculptor approached
the complexity of his subject; yet no one fails
to see the life and spirit of the man.

The secret of this serenity and simplicity
without loss to the vitality of his subject is the
sculptor's secret. It is possible to go but a very
little way in describing his method. One can
say that the type is never taken from any one
model but shapes itself gradually in his imagi-

[118]

nation after he has seen hundreds or even thousands of individuals who in one way or another contribute to his ideal. This is not like a modern " composite photograph," for that is mechanical and repeats only points of likeness between the faces it combines; it is not like the " Pantheia " of Lucian, that ideal statue combining the lips of one statue, the cheeks of another, and the eyes of another, features that in each case have won the approbation of the public; it is a new personality, an individual of universal significance, created by the artist. Yet the result is representation, ideal representation, for the artist's aim is to produce a figure such as one might meet any day in the streets of the city, only more perfect. To accomplish his end he omits what is irrelevant to his purpose and emphasizes what is relevant. Nothing casual or accidental is admissible; everything is left out which does not help to make visible his fundamental idea. In fact the artist may abbreviate nature as much as he chooses, as in early Greek painting where only flat color was used and no effort was made for perspective. In red-figured vase paintings of the severe period, and in the white lekythoi where a plain colored wash for the garments supplements the glaze outlines of the figure, very few lines are sufficient to present the artist's theme. The abbreviation of nature is carried to a great extent in all Greek sculpture, particularly in the fifth century B.C., though the sculptor never fails to give animation to the broad, simple modelling by means of a subtle differentiation of the surface. In a word, the artist omits as much of visible fact as he chooses or as his mode of work demands, in order to emphasize his conception of the subject. He deals with a universal that is individual and concrete, in contrast with the abstract universals of science. The Greek painting or statue is so infused with the idea that it may seem even more real than the object represented. Such is the goal of idealistic representation.

V

FINALLY, the art of Greece may be called organic. That is to say, the painting or statue or decorated utensil is so constructed that every part is adjusted to the whole just as if it were an organic growth. The living being is one structure of interdependent parts because it has grown up under the control of one life principle

[120]

within; similarly the Greek work of art, though it gives only the outward form in its lines and surfaces, seems to have been constructed from within outward to make visible the physical and mental life of its subject.

The Greek sense for order is at least a prerequisite for this result. The present-day revolt from tradition in the arts, as well as in other phases of human thought and activity, makes it difficult to consider sympathetically the Greek point of view. Our poets, for example, scorning the Victorian era, have developed *vers libre* which, though without a fixed metrical scheme, has at its best melody and poetic thought and exactness of language. But even the verse of Shakespeare and of our best English lyricists avoids the severe form of the odes of Sappho and the choral passages of Aeschylus. The organic unity of the Greek ode, in which rigid form is made simply the perfect vehicle for thought and feeling, is typical of Greek art. The controlling principle of Greek architecture is the sense for order manifesting itself in recurring rhythm and in a harmonious unity. Palaeontologists have claimed the ability to reconstruct some extinct animal from a single bone; similarly, a fragment of some moulding or the piece of a capital may enable the student to reconstruct with reasonable accuracy the temple from which it came, so organic is the structure of the Greek temple.

In the representative arts of sculpture and painting the manifestation of the sense for order is of course far more subtle. With their innate fondness for number it was natural for Greek sculptors to seek a modulus and to construct their figures by simple multiples of this amount (see p. 52). The modulus, however, gives only one dimension after another in the framework of the figure. In drawing on bases, in reliefs, and in the early sculpture which was meant to be seen only from the front, the two-dimensional design is developed with a symmetry and balance, a rhythm and harmony, which have no numerical equivalents. Each line takes its place in a pattern of which it is an organic part, that is each line seems to be determined by the whole to which it belongs; the result is a vital organic unity. Take for example the so-called " Birth of Aphrodite " (Plate XV*b*). Two crouching women stand on stony slopes, their arms outstretched to help up the young woman in the center, before

[122]

whose waist they hold a garment. The spring-
ing pose as they lean forward, the rhythmic
lines of their garments, broken only by the
drawn-back foot, the interplay of the extended
arms, all lead the eye up and in toward the central figure. The balance is free from mechanical rigidity, yet is carefully studied; every line
takes its place in a pattern designed to emphasize the sculptor's theme, a pattern that
centers on the head of the rising goddess.

With the gradual development of three-
dimensional design the sense for order is mani-
fested in an increasingly complex manner. The
pattern of the outline changes from moment to
moment as an observer walks around the statue.
The Discobolus is really effective only from
one point of view. The Doryphorus may be
seen from front or back but it is not effective
from the sides, and even the Hermes loses in
design from certain points; it is only in the
work of Lysippus that organic unity of design
is so developed that the outline is equally significant of the artist's meaning from every point
of view. But the design of the outline is not
the primary interest of sculpture in the round.
It is the subtle balance and harmony of the
surface planes, surfaces that combine the sim-

plicity of the artist's idea with the complex curves of the human figure, which lend character to the Greek statue.

The significance of organic unity in Greek sculpture may be made clearer by a comparison of two heads in Boston. The terracotta head of a Roman from the period of the early empire (Plate XVI*b*) is so literal a presentation of the subject that some critics have even suggested it was based on a cast from life. The furrowed face, the sagging flesh of cheeks and neck, the compressed lips drawn down at the ends, the thin prominent nose, all these are unique forms due to the man's nature and his reactions to life. Expressive as it is, distinguished as the man was, it has the organic unity of nature not of art. It is like a three-dimensional photograph, if such a thing were possible, repeating just what a camera might give. A striking contrast is offered by the so-called head from Chios (Plate XVI*a*). No human head ever showed this " divine geometry in its balance of volumes," to use Rodin's phrase in describing it. The face is an ovoid of the proportion five to three, and the top of the head would be almost a half sphere of the smaller of these diameters, with the result that a horizontal section through the middle of the forehead would approximate to a circle. The lines along the flat ridge of the nose rise straight, turn in a quarter circle, and then run nearly straight along the sharply marked eyebrows. The edge of the hair along the forehead is a simple geometric curve, not to speak of the simple lines of eye and mouth, or the studied simplicity of the planes of the cheek. The full significance of the design is not clear, for presumably the missing parts of the top of the head mean that a veil was attached, covering the back of the head; but as it stands, it is almost a geometric design, yet so close to nature that the geometry only lends force and clarity to the sensitive sweetness of the face. Is it Persephone, the beloved daughter, who descends to the realm of Hades each year, only to be restored to Demeter with the sprouting vegetation? Certainly it is a goddess, no human girl. The structure of the head is as truly organic, as clearly the expression of a life principle within, as in the case of the Roman terracotta head, but none of the accidents of human growth are present. Every detail, every least modulation of the surface, is determined by the Greek sense for order. The artist has created a being so purified of all that might mar its perfection, yet so marked by all the insignia of life, that it seems almost more real than any product of natural growth. It has the organic structure of art, not of nature.

Is it possible to go farther in explaining the effect sought and achieved by this sense of order? From its earliest beginnings and in every land art has one characteristic, namely, that it depends on design to fulfil its purpose. Whether the design is made up of abstract forms, or, as in Minoan art, of forms drawn from nature, the result is felt to be art, if the design makes its direct appeal to the observer. The distinction of Greek art is that it successfully combines subtle design with true representation, that progressive vision and technique are accompanied step by step by increasingly effective design, that the artist consistently aims to present both what he sees and what he feels in a manner to carry both his vision and his emotion to those for whom he works.

How a work of art produces a feeling of exaltation or thrills of satisfaction is no simple question. It is clear, however, that one factor in reproducing the emotion of the artist through his work is the design or pattern, that combination of lines or surfaces or volumes which the artist creates. For architecture it is clear that the " rightness " which satisfies the mind depends first on the proportions of the whole and then on the design which in detail enriches and reënforces the effect of the whole. Practically the same statement holds good for a Greek vase of bronze or pottery, or for a piece of jewelry. Sculpture and painting are more like poetry, in that it is the function of effective design to reënforce the idea presented in the language of poetry or in the visible form of a statue. With the great range of sound material available for the poet, variations of accent and length of syllables and quality of syllables, he produces a sound-pattern as the vehicle for the emotion which attends his thought. Similarly, the painter or the sculptor creates a design which fulfils the same purpose. To recur to the " Birth of Aphrodite " (p. 122), the curving lines to be supplied at the bottom of the relief, repeated in the garment held before the rising goddess and again in the backs of the crouching nymphs, not only are parts of an organic design but also they emphasize the tender solicitude of the nymphs; the diagonal lines of the arms make one feel the motion of the goddess upward; the very lines of the hair on the central head contribute to the feeling of life in her attitude. In the Discobolus (Plate XIII*a*) the feeling of a coiled spring is given immediately by the pattern of the lines, a feeling which lends new meaning to the figure for it induces an " empathy " in the observer. And in the Nike of Paeonius (UPA, pl. 110), does not everyone recognize that, even though the wings are missing, this solid form of a young woman is just floating down to earth? The representation of limbs that bear no weight and the slightly forward poise of the figure against the wind which blows back her garments, help to suggest the idea; but it is only the magic of the design which obliges one to feel that this goddess is really poised in the air.

It is difficult to describe or even suggest in words the full significance of the organic structure of a work of art. That a statue or painting is conceived through the aesthetic sense of order, that it has a vital organic unity, that this unity is really a creation of the artist, may be clear; but how the artist uses his design to convey his emotion to others is something that defies analysis. If only one's emotion is stirred before a statue in a manner that deepens the meaning of the figure, the experience may be accepted as the highest achievement of the sculptor. The combination of true representation with effective design has assumed most varied forms in succeeding centuries, but the Greek way has left its indelible stamp on the aim and method of later European art.

ANY attempt to assay the influence of Greece on the art of the west and to determine its extent in detail would involve writing a history of art in Europe and America. The present sketch can only indicate the directions in which to look for this influence. That many of the types and methods developed in Greece have persisted to the present time is shown by even a casual examination of the subject. Our debt to Greece, however, lies far deeper. The motivating spirit of art, its nature and its significance are still moulded by this inheritance.

All the great periods of art in Europe have been characterized by a communal interest in artistic endeavor and by progressive growth in a sound tradition, in contrast with revolt from the past on the one hand and mere repetition of outworn forms on the other. In general, these conditions have no connection with the influence of Greece, although in the Renaissance that influence was paramount. On the other hand, Greek humanism had continued as a living force in Europe. In the Roman world art was concerned with men and their achievements, and it was at its best in portraits. In the church art of the early centuries, of the Romanesque period, and of the Gothic period, sculptors loved to stress the humanity of Mother and Child and of prophets and saints, though humanism itself was quite in the background of men's thought. The revival of the Greek point of view in the Renaissance brought into the foreground that attention to man as man and to his daily life, which has characterized the art not only of that period but also of all succeeding periods. It may be a far cry from Praxiteles to Michelangelo, to Vermeer and Rembrandt, to Millet, but the interest in man which marked the work of the former equally underlies the work of the later artists. The humanism of our western art is inherited from Greece, and is not found outside the sphere of Greek influence.

Representation of objects as seen, the key-

note of later European art, is also a legacy from
Greece. It met the approval of the practical
Roman mind, which explored new avenues in
this field; it was passed on to the early church;
Byzantine art in the west was modified by its
influence; in the Romanesque and Gothic periods it produced a sculpture and stained glass
which through their reality and their charm
incidentally served a didactic purpose. In the
Renaissance it was the task of painter and
sculptor to represent Madonna or saints or alle-
gorical figures, scenes from sacred legend or
from daily life, or persons who were their pa-
trons, with all the fidelity to truth which was in
their power. They sought to capture the truth
of vision in form and color; it was the truth of
reality for them, but a reality nobler and purer
than what men had seen before the artist set
it before them; their aim was representation
with the realism and the idealism of Greece. In
later Europe knowledge of the artist's problems
has increased, even if the freshness of attack is
gone; his subjects have varied and his interest
has shifted now toward that of the scientist,
now toward that of the seer; nevertheless (until the revolt in recent years) his goal has consistently been an art of representation. This

conception of the function of art is part of our debt to Greece.

Finally, the principle of organic structure in our art owes much to the Greeks. Of course the meaning of design was not a new discovery in Greece; it is recognized everywhere, and in fact it has probably been better understood in the orient than even in the west; but the use of design to reënforce representation began with Greece. The failure of this procedure was the weakness of Roman art. It was through Byzantium that this phase of the Greek achievement was brought to Europe, to stir the souls of men by religious painting and sculpture in the so-called Dark Ages. But it was only in the Renaissance that representation governed by organic design in the Greek manner came again to its own. This practice has remained as the basis of our art. Representation that was true because it had the vital organic unity of art, that made an emotional appeal because of the design which intensified its meaning, has been the aim of our painting and sculpture in these later centuries. It is the mark of Greece on our art.

It is customary for critics and historians of European art to stress an antithesis between the classical tradition on the one hand and on the other hand romanticism or naturalism or some other trend. For example, Chapu may be called a classicist, Rodin a romanticist, Meunier a realist. The antithesis is justified only to the extent to which even in art of a high order the details of indebtedness to Greece are partially suppressed by the artist's sensitiveness to a totally different age. However, with our increasing knowledge of original Greek art we must recognize that our debt to Greece is not confined to any one school or tendency of western art. Rodin no less than Chapu was a devoted student of classical art, and Meunier sought to catch the spirit of Greece in his work. Of course Greek influence is sometimes clear, sometimes obscured in later Europe as new forces have made themselves felt from outside, or have developed from within under the stress of social and economic and political changes. The ideas to be expressed in painting and sculpture have been profoundly modified, and new forms of expression have been developed to meet new demands. Nevertheless, the fact remains that our civilization has almost universally accepted the conception of art, its method, and its significance, which was passed on to us from ancient Greece. One school has succeeded another since the Renaissance, but all have drawn their inspiration from one source, all have followed the path first trodden in Greece.

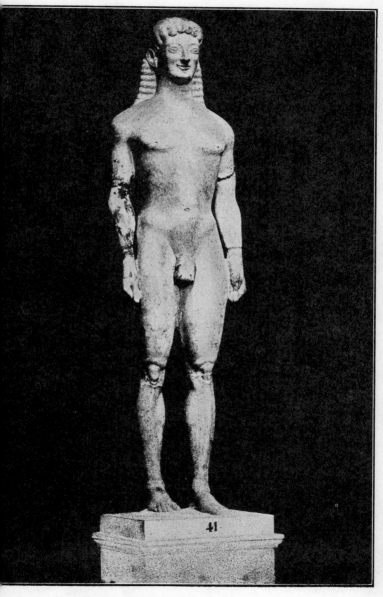

PLATE I. " Apollo " of Tenea

58

PLATE III. Athena Lemnia

PLATE IV. Hermes of Praxiteles

PLATE V. Nike of Samothrace

PLATE XV. Tube of Dionysus.

PLATE VII. Peasant Woman

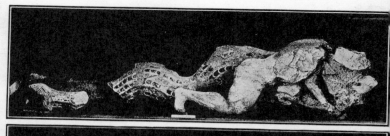

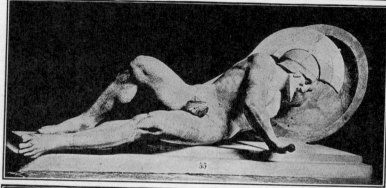

PLATE VIII. (a) *top*, Heracles and the Triton
(b) *middle*, Wounded warrior from Aegina pediment
(c) *bottom*, "Theseus" from the East Parthenon pediment

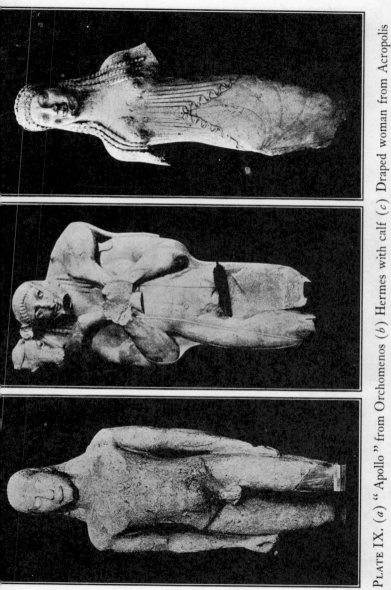

PLATE IX. (*a*) "Apollo" from Orchomenos (*b*) Hermes with calf (*c*) Draped woman from Acropolis

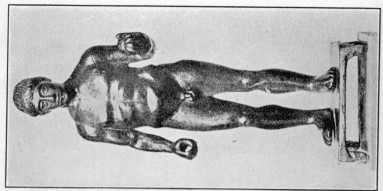

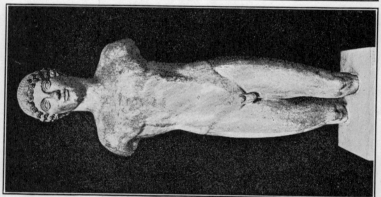

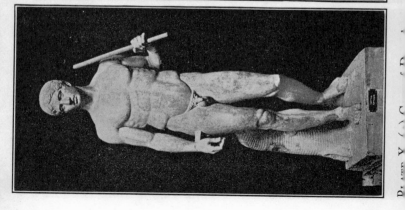

PLATE X (A) Statues of Poseidon, and of Ephebus and ...

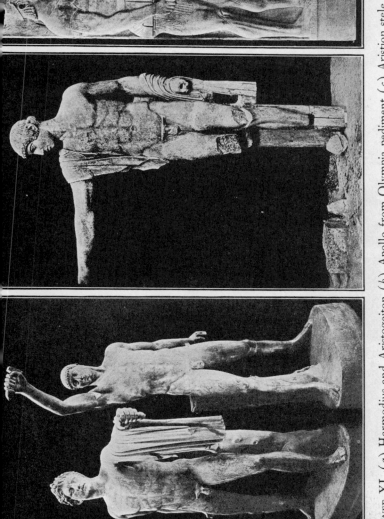

PLATE XI. (a) Harmodius and Aristogeiton (b) Apollo from Olympia pediment (c) Aristion stele

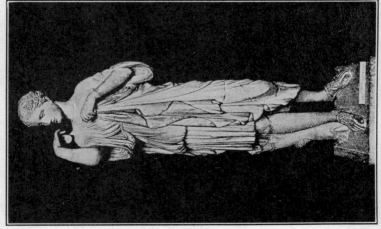

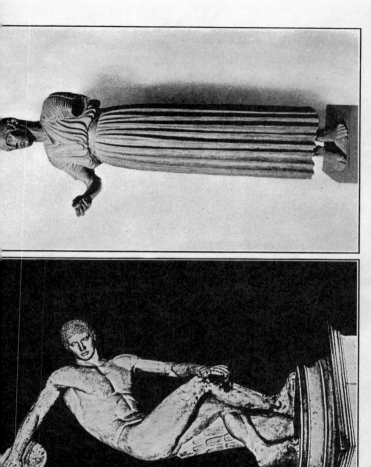

PLATE XIII. (*a*) Copy of Discobolus of Myron (*b*) Charioteer from Delphi

PLATE XV. (a) *above*, Hegeso stele
(b) *below*, " Birth of Aphrodite "

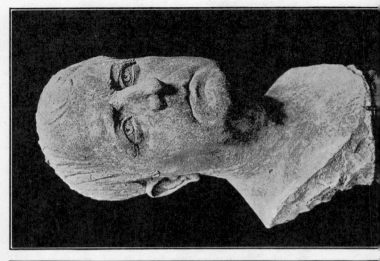

BIBLIOGRAPHY

Greek Art:

CARPENTER, RHYS, *The Esthetic Basis of Greek Art.* New York, 1921.

COLLIGNON, MAX, *Histoire de la sculpture grecque.* Paris, 1892, 1897.

GARDNER, E. A., *Handbook of Greek Sculpture.* London, 1898.

GARDNER, PERCY, *Principles of Greek Art.* New York, 1914.

RICHTER, G. M. A., *The Sculptors and Sculpture of the Greeks.* New Haven, 1929.

SWINDLER, M. H., *Ancient Painting.* New Haven, Conn., 1929.

TARBELL, F. B., *History of Greek Art.* London, 1896.

UNIVERSITY PRINTS, Series A, Greek and Roman Sculpture. Boston, 1916.

WALTERS, H. B., *The Art of the Greeks.* London, 1906.

Greek Art, Influence of:

ADAMS, HERBERT, "The Debt of Modern Sculpture to Ancient Greece," in *Art and Archaeology,* XIII. 218–221 (1921).

AGARD, W. R., *The Greek Tradition in Sculpture.* Baltimore, 1930.

BERTRAND, L., *La fin du classicisme et le retour à l'antique en France.* Paris, 1897.

DEONNA, "L'imitation de l'antique par quelques artistes représentés au Musée du Genève," in *Bulletin du Musée d'art et d'histoire,* Genève, I, pp. 152 ff.

GARDNER, PERCY, "The Lamps of Greek Art," in *The Legacy of Greece.* Oxford, 1922.

SIRÉN, O., "The Importance of the Antique to Donatello," in *American Journal of Archaeology*, XVIII. 438–461 (1914).

TREU, GEORG, *Hellenistische Stimmungen in der Bildhauerei von Einst und Jetzt*. Leipzig, 1910.

Indian Art:

COOMARASWAMY, A. K., *History of Indian and Indonesian Art*. New York, 1927.

Chinese and Japanese Art:

OKAKURA, K., *Ideals of the East*. London, 1903.

SIRÉN, O., *Chinese Sculpture*. London, 1925.

Our Debt to Greece and Rome

AUTHORS AND TITLES

AUTHORS AND TITLES

HOMER. *John A. Scott.*

SAPPHO. *David M. Robinson.*

EURIPIDES. *F. L. Lucas.*

ARISTOPHANES. *Louis E. Lord.*

DEMOSTHENES. *Charles D. Adams.*

THE POETICS OF ARISTOTLE. *Lane Cooper.*

GREEK RHETORIC AND LITERARY CRITICISM. *W. Rhys Roberts.*

LUCIAN. *Francis G. Allinson.*

CICERO AND HIS INFLUENCE. *John C. Rolfe.*

CATULLUS. *Karl P. Harrington.*

LUCRETIUS AND HIS INFLUENCE. *George Depue Hadzsits.*

OVID. *Edward Kennard Rand.*

HORACE. *Grant Showerman.*

VIRGIL. *John William Mackail.*

SENECA THE PHILOSOPHER. *Richard Mott Gummere.*

APULEIUS. *Elizabeth Hazelton Haight.*

MARTIAL. *Paul Nixon.*

PLATONISM. *Alfred Edward Taylor.*

ARISTOTELIANISM. *John L. Stocks.*

STOICISM. *Robert Mark Wenley.*

LANGUAGE AND PHILOLOGY. *Roland G. Kent.*

AUTHORS AND TITLES

AESCHYLUS AND SOPHOCLES.   *J. T. Sheppard.*

GREEK RELIGION.   *Walter Woodburn Hyde.*

SURVIVALS OF ROMAN RELIGION.   *Gordon J. Laing.*

MYTHOLOGY.   *Jane Ellen Harrison.*

ANCIENT BELIEFS IN THE IMMORTALITY OF THE SOUL.   *Clifford H. Moore.*

STAGE ANTIQUITIES.   *James Turney Allen.*

PLAUTUS AND TERENCE.   *Gilbert Norwood.*

ROMAN POLITICS.   *Frank Frost Abbott.*

PSYCHOLOGY, ANCIENT AND MODERN.   *G. S. Brett.*

ANCIENT AND MODERN ROME.   *Rodolfo Lanciani.*

WARFARE BY LAND AND SEA.   *Eugene S. McCartney.*

THE GREEK FATHERS.   *James Marshall Campbell.*

GREEK BIOLOGY AND MEDICINE.   *Henry Osborn Taylor.*

MATHEMATICS.   *David Eugene Smith.*

LOVE OF NATURE AMONG THE GREEKS AND ROMANS.   *H. R. Fairclough.*

ANCIENT WRITING AND ITS INFLUENCE.   *B. L. Ullman.*

GREEK ART.   *Arthur Fairbanks.*

ARCHITECTURE.   *Alfred M. Brooks.*

ENGINEERING.   *Alexander P. Gest.*

MODERN TRAITS IN OLD GREEK LIFE.   *Charles Burton Gulick.*

ROMAN PRIVATE LIFE.   *Walton Brooks McDaniel.*

GREEK AND ROMAN FOLKLORE.   *William Reginald Halliday.*

ANCIENT EDUCATION.   *J. F. Dobson.*